Move Along; Nothing to See Here

Darrell McMann

Copyright © Darrell McMann

All rights reserved.

ISBN: 1453658769

ISBN-13: 9781453658765

Chapter 1

I started the hiring process for the Mobile Police Department in the summer of 1990, as one of several thousand applicants. The first step was the entrance examination for the police academy, which was given over a one-week period. I arrived early on the day I was scheduled to take it, so I had plenty of time to check out my competition. I wondered why some people would show up for a police academy entrance examination or any other exam for a career, looking like they had slept in their clothes and hadn't bothered to bathe before leaving the house. I couldn't believe how many people couldn't follow simple directions and showed up several minutes late.

I passed the entrance examination, and I know that surprised more than a few people. The department then scheduled a physical examination, physical fitness test, psychological examination, polygraph, background check, interview, and drug screening. After I had been an officer on the street for a couple of years, I wondered how reliable the psychological examination was when I talked to some of my fellow officers. Someone, who I'm sure was highly paid, compiled all this information and gave everyone a ranking. I was ninety-second on the hiring list.

I was discouraged when I received notification of my ranking because I knew the department was only scheduling two academy classes the following year with sixteen trainees in each class. I was informed that I shouldn't let it discourage me because the department usually went through fifty applicants to find sixteen who successfully passed all the phases of the hiring process. I was told that it was likely that I would be in the second class; so I would have to keep working until my number came up.

The second police academy class of 1991 began on June 10, 1991 without me. I was extremely disappointed but would try again when the city started accepting applications later in the year.

Move Along; Nothing to See Here

On June 11, the training sergeant at the police academy telephoned to inform me that two people had quit on the first day; he asked if I was still interested. I told him I was, and he told me my first day would be June 17, and he gave me a list of things I would need.

Six days later I reported for my first day at the police academy—I was so stoked, I arrived half an hour early. I met with the training sergeant and most of the academy staff. They made me feel comfortable and told me to come to them if I had any problems. The sergeant escorted me and the other new trainee to a classroom, where we waited for our physical training instructor.

When Corporal Jerry Greer entered the room sporting a large maniacal grin, I knew he wasn't there to make me feel comfortable. He did say good morning, but I knew he didn't mean it.

Cpl. Greer believed in running. We ran five miles on Mondays, three miles on Wednesdays, and we ran one and one-half miles to Ladd Stadium on Fridays. We would run the bleachers on all four sides of the stadium and then run back to the police academy. He believed a cop should be in good physical shape to defend himself. A cop who is in good physical condition is less likely to be assaulted. Cpl. Greer was an ex-marine, so we would chant things like "Mobile PD kickin' ass PD," while he ran. We got a lot of strange looks when we ran through the Maysville community. The neighborhood and the police department didn't have a healthy relationship at the time.

Over the next sixteen weeks, we had classes in criminal law, city ordinances, traffic law, officer safety, CPR, blood-borne pathogens, policies and procedures, and many other topics that were incredibly boring. I found the policies and procedures extremely interesting. The instructor would remind us every so often that these were just guidelines and that circumstances might occur that would prevent you from following procedures. We would discover if you didn't follow the guidelines and things went wrong, you would get hung out to dry for violating policies and procedures.

Darrell McMann

Representatives from the local departments of health, human resources, mental health; the Council for the Aging; domestic violence advocates; juvenile justice advocates, MADD, child and elderly abuse advocates, animal control, and many other entities outside the police department give presentations. They all preached the same message—we are here to support you. They urged us to call them if we needed their help or expertise, and they said someone would come. That wasn't quite true. You learn quickly that if you call, they won't be able to find anyone to come.

Cpl. Greer was our main instructor, and his specialty was officer safety. He showed us videos of officers who were killed or hurt because of poor officer safety. He instructed us on weapon retention, disarming people with knives and guns, pressure points, ground fighting, and the department's guidelines for use of force. We had scenarios that were supposed to be designed for the trainee to win if he did everything right—we never won a scenario. Cpl. Greer shoved a blueberry muffin in my face when I was the investigating officer on a suspicious person complaint. He said, "You see that! That's your blood and brains scattered all over the ground! Are you sure you want this job? Maybe you should go back to doing what you did before you came here!" I was extremely pissed off, but I replayed what happened in my mind and remembered the lesson.

He also liked to give pop quizzes. He would ask, "How many calls involving guns does an individual officer respond to during a shift?" We threw out some numbers and percentages but couldn't come up with the right answer. The answer is every call you go on. *You* bring it, and that's why weapon retention is so important. Someone asked, "What percentage of officers who are shot are shot with their own gun?" He said, "I don't know but it's too many."

During our time at the academy, we were able to go out and ride along with a patrol officer. I rode with Wade Brantley in the Third Precinct, which covers the east side of I65 and the north side of Airport Boulevard to Government Street, and continuing along the north side of Government to Broad Street. Covering the west side of Broad

Move Along; Nothing to See Here

Street to the Mobile River. The northern boundary was the city limits. The precinct also covers the Happy Hills, Orange Grove, and Roger Williams housing projects and the neighborhoods of Magazine, Toulminville, Trinity Gardens, Crichton, and the Bottoms.

Wade asked me if I had ever been to this side of town. I told him I hadn't. He said, "Prepare for your eyes to be opened," while he was loading an extended spare magazine for his Glock 17. I thought, "Oh great, he's crazy!" I decided he was perfectly sane or close to it after we responded to about four or five shots-fired calls that shift.

I will never forget the last call we answered that night. A guy called 911 and said he heard a baby crying. Wade knocked on the door to the complainants' apartment. The door opened, and we heard a voice tell us to come in. The apartment was dark, so Wade surveyed the room with his flashlight and told me not touch anything. He turned on the living room ceiling light. The complainant asked him to turn it off because it hurt his eyes. The guy was wearing an adult diaper; he had open sores all over his body and was scratching them. The floor was covered with napkins he had dabbed his sores with. He said he heard a baby crying inside the walls and wanted us to find the baby. He kept coming toward us, and we kept backing away. Wade called the paramedics to take him to the hospital. When we got back in the cruiser to leave Wade asked me if I was sure I wanted this job. I didn't answer.

The day before graduation Cpl. Greer told us to look at each other. He said there are fifteen of you. Within five years, one or two of you will be dead, two of will decide being a cop isn't worth it, one or two of you will be fired or resign before you're fired, and two or three of you will take jobs with another department. He went on to say if one us got someone he likes hurt or killed because our head was up our ass, then we will have to answer to him. He told us several times that we would lose our old friends because they didn't want to be around a cop. He said, "You will change. Some of your old friends won't like the new you. You spend all your off duty time with other cops." That does come true for some people.

During my time at the academy, my mom introduced me to my future wife, Kim. She had a part-time position in my mom's office. She was very supportive and thought it was pretty neat that I was in the police academy. She had put herself through school and worked three part-time jobs to pay off her student loans. I hung around a lot with a group of guys from class. They had their wives and girlfriends with them and didn't believe I was seeing anyone. I introduced Kim to them before the graduation ceremony. While waiting behind the stage, I was accused of paying this Kim girl off. It was too convenient for her to show up after all this time. Kim had a great sense of humor and knew what she wanted out of life. Once she was focused on something, she would do whatever it took to get it done.

I met her parents a few months after we started dating. She told me later her mother said, "Cops cheat on and beat their wives." I was wearing a pair of faded jeans when I met her. She told Kim she didn't like my jeans. I said, "I don't care. I am not dating your mother." I would find out later how wrong I was.

September 27, 1991 is a day that will forever be etched in the annals of the history of law enforcement. Well, not really, but it sounds good, and it *was* a big day for me. That was graduation day from the Mobile Police Academy, marking the beginning of my law enforcement career. The chief of police, Ray Nagin, spoke eloquently about the history of law enforcement and our futures as Mobile police officers. We were told he informed a prior graduating class that they would be the first police officers fighting crime in outer space. Most people thought he had already spent way too much time without sufficient oxygen, but I digress. The chief called our names one by one, shook our hands, congratulated us, posed for a photo op, and then handed each one of us our certifications. I was daydreaming during his wonderful speech and his personal words of encouragement so I don't recall anything he said.

Once an officer graduates from the police academy, he is assigned to the Field Training Program, which runs for another twelve weeks. There were three phases of four weeks. Every four weeks, you went

Move Along; Nothing to See Here

to a different field training officer. (FTO) The department added four weeks since it was close to Thanksgiving and Christmas. We rotated walking tours with a fellow rookie downtown and at the malls.

Billy Flounder, one of my academy classmates, and I were assigned to one of the malls on a Saturday toward the end of our walking-tour rotation the day of the 1991 Alabama-Auburn game. We walked into one of the shoe stores, and I was looking around because I needed a new pair sneakers. One of the associates was wearing an Alabama sweater, and his coworker was wearing an Auburn sweater. The associate wearing the Alabama sweater greeted us and asked what we were up to. I jokingly said, "Oh just looking for an Auburn fan to harass." The Auburn associate took exception to that and told me he would sue me if I harassed him. His coworker and I told him I was just kidding. He wouldn't let it go and told me he was going to sue and would see me in court. I decided to ignore him and motioned for Billy to come with me. As we were walking out of the store, the associate continued to tell me he was going to sue me. Billy had had enough. He turned around and said, "Go ahead and sue him, big mouth. He loves court." I thanked him later and reminded him neither one of us had been in court yet.

My first FTO, Cathy, was in the Fourth Precinct which covered the westside of I65 north of Airport Boulevard to the city limits. One of the first calls we responded to was at a trailer park off of Moffett Road. When we arrived, the complainant walked up to us and pointed to a small fifth wheel trailer. She said she heard what she thought was a muffled explosion and then heard a scream. She said, "A little guy ran out and looked like he was shaking like a dog when it's wet. He went back in after a minute or two and hasn't come out."

We walked over to the trailer to investigate. We were almost overcome by the noxious fumes coming from it. I could see someone through the window looking at me, so I motioned for him to come outside. The guy was about five-feet-two, and his eyes looked like they were going pop out of his head. I asked him if he was okay and I asked him to explain the fumes. He told me he was fine; one of the

Darrell McMann

propane tanks in the trailer was leaking. Cathy called for paramedics, and I told him to open all the windows and prop open the door to ventilate the trailer.

A couple of neighbors motioned for Cathy to come speak to them; I stayed with the little guy. When the fire department arrived, I walked over to advise them of what was going on and to have them check out little guy. I turned to walk back to the trailer with the fire captain and realized little guy had gone back in and was closing the windows. We tried to open the door and realized he had locked it. The fire captain and I were trying to talk to him through the window; he was sitting in a chair with his back to us. He turned to face us, and he had a lighter in one hand and a propane tank in his lap. He smiled, and the fire captain yelled, "RUN!"

We evacuated the residents of the trailer park and requested the SWAT team. The crisis negotiator attempted to get him to come out for about two and one-half hours, but the little guy was ignoring him. The sniper could see him huffing propane every few minutes.

Little guy was watching the 10:00 news, when he realized the reporter was standing at the entrance to his trailer park. He suddenly ran out of the trailer toward Moffett Road screaming, "MOMMA MOMMA!" Cathy and I tackled him before he could get too far; he put up a fight, but we got control of him quickly. When we stood him up, he kept saying he needed to check on momma. He thought the news was reporting a bad traffic accident, and his momma was hurt.

My second FTO was Bart Mathews. Bart was assigned to the Second Precinct, which covered the area west of I 65 south of Airport Blvd to the city limits. Bart enjoyed driving while I attempted to write reports. Bart's driving was terrible, so it took me extra time to complete a report. Bart would point randomly in the opposite direction I happened to be looking and say, "You didn't see that?" I would say, "No what did you see?" He would say, "Never mind," and sigh.

Move Along; Nothing to See Here

We went to a disturbance at an apartment complex on Azalea Road. It was my first call that involved a gun that I didn't bring with me. The complainant gave dispatch the apartment number the suspect was seen entering. A sergeant walked up to me just before we went up the stairs. He slapped me on the back and said, "It's all yours." I wasn't sure what he meant at first, but I figured it out when he said, "Well, what in the hell are you waiting for?" I went up the stairs. I got to the apartment and listened before I knocked. The sergeant said to Bart, "He isn't as dumb as he looks."

I heard several people inside the apartment; they didn't sound like they were arguing, they were talking about going to the movies. I knocked on the door, and a female opened the door, took one look at us, and then tried to shut it again. The sergeant stuck his flashlight in the doorframe, and I pushed it open.

There were two guys in the apartment who looked like they wanted to run but didn't. I told them to put their hands behind their heads and patted them down, but we didn't find any guns in the apartment. I asked the female why she tried to close the door on us. She said, "Police make me nervous." We found out that one of the guys had an ex-girlfriend who lived in the same apartment complex as his new girlfriend. She called to get even with him. We went to her apartment but she wasn't home.

I made a traffic stop one night on a vehicle with an expired tag. The driver had an expired driver license, and she didn't have a car seat for her three-year-old. The driver, a female, began crying while I was talking with her. I felt like a giant heel; she lived down the street, so I sent her home. When I got back in the cruiser Bart asked me why she was leaving, and why didn't I write any tickets. I told him she started crying. He smiled and said, "I can't believe you fell for it. Were there any tears?" I said, "NO," and put the car in drive. "Where are you going?" he asked. "To give her some tickets," I replied. He said, "Let her go, you've embarrassed yourself enough already."

Darrell McMann

I had a two-week period between the second and third phases of the FTO program when I was assigned downtown for a walking beat. Lilly Heath, Lonnie Wilson, and I were assigned to Corporal Wesley Snipes for two weeks that went by quickly and for the most part, uneventful. I spent the second week trying to keep Lilly from being alone with Cpl. Snipes. She told me he was trying to get close to her, and she was afraid he was going to ask her out. I could tell he was getting annoyed that I was always around. A half hour before the end of our shift he called her on the radio and asked her to come meet him. She told me I better not leave her alone. I thought it was funny; she didn't. I told her I wouldn't leave, and I knew it would give me a chance to annoy someone just by standing there and not speaking.

When we arrived, I could tell by the look on his face that Cpl. Snipes wasn't happy I was with her. He made it obvious he wanted to speak to Lilly only. He took a few steps backward and motioned for her to join him. He started talking, and I took a few steps toward them. The look on his face was priceless. If he could have pulled his gun and shot me, he would have. He moved again three or four other times, and I would join them or get within five feet of them. I must have been good at acting like I didn't have a clue what he was trying to do.

When our shift was over he looked at me and told me I could go home. I told him I enjoyed working with him and hoped I would work with him again in the future. He said he enjoyed working with me and waited for me to leave, but I kept standing there. Lilly didn't know what to do. She finally told him she had to go because I had to give her a ride. He said, "Okay," and we left. I laughed until my sides hurt, but Lilly didn't think it was very funny.

My third FTO, Charles, was assigned to the Third Precinct, and we were on the midnight shift. Charles told me the first night to bring a pillow; he believed in sleeping on the midnight shift. We answered a disturbance call in Trinity Gardens the night after Christmas at about 2:00 A.M.; there were about ten to fifteen people in the front yard when

Move Along; Nothing to See Here

we got there all looking toward the house. The complainant told the dispatcher that thirty people were involved, so two other cars also with trainees were sent to the call.

A female in the house began screaming and cursing at someone outside. Charles and I went inside to find out what was going on. There were several more people in the house arguing. The female was pretty aggravated, and she kept screaming and cursing. The person she was screaming at got the message and ran in the house to confront her along with five or six other people. Charles and I were in the middle of the brawl trying to separate everybody. After being kicked and punched several times, we quickly changed tactics. We had to defend ourselves. The other officers called for additional units and started throwing people out of the house. We eventually got control and found the instigator, who was bleeding, hiding behind a chair.

Being evaluated closely every day for three months can get tiresome. You have to constantly be aware of where you are. You have to give your location when answering dispatch. You also have to know what the officers around you are doing and where they are in case they need help. You have to constantly be focused on officer safety. One minor slip up will get you a bad rating and possibly get you or someone else hurt or killed. It's important to ensure that you've gotten all the pertinent information necessary for a report, and then you have to write a good report. My best advice is to listen to everything a witness and suspect says, know criminal and traffic laws, and watch for suspicious people and hundreds of other things while being evaluated every second. You have to realize that everyone doesn't tell the truth. You had to know where you were all the time; if you were asked and didn't know, you would get a response like "I'm glad I'm not lying in the street bleeding and hoping you will help me."

You learn the order of the streets in the beats you work and which streets have the fewest stop signs. You ride with your window down, so you can hear what's going on. I was amazed at the things I heard at 2:00 A.M. and 3:00 A.M.—gunshots and people arguing. You learn not to park in front of the address to which you were dispatched to avoid being ambushed; it's safer to park two or three houses away. When you knock on the door, you don't stand directly in front of the door if you can help it. I learned to knock and back away quickly. You never know what to expect when the door opens. I hate small porches with recessed doors. You learn to check the windows and the yard as you approach a house. I was surprised one night by a guy sitting in a car in the driveway. I walked by the car and was about to knock on the door, when he got out and asked me what I needed. From that point on, I looked in every car on my way to the door.

Report writing is obviously extremely important. Officers have various opinions about what to include in a report and the writing style to use for a report. I decided from the beginning to include everything I could in a report. Some officers purposely omit a few facts from their reports. They do that because they don't want the defense attorney to have all the facts. I don't understand that line of thinking; they tend to spend a lot of time in court. When they are testifying and are asked a question that should have been addressed in the report, they have to think about an answer. It could appear they don't know and are trying to come up with an answer. I write in plain English and explain exactly what happened, including what was said if it's important. Some officers use legal-sounding words and words that sound intelligent. Problem with that is they don't use them correctly. They try to use the words when they testify hoping to sound smart, but it usually has the opposite affect.

You learn terms such as skunk molley, alley bat, tranny, hair bag, dirt bag, skell, thug, skint back, apin ass, rollin dirty, and all the street names for the different types of drugs. Skunk molley is the name given to prostitutes and or crack heads that haven't showered in several days. Alley Bat is a prostitute who is so ugly she should be hanging upside down in an alley waiting for her dates. Tranny is short for Transvestite. Hair bag, dirt bag, skell, thug, and other more colorful names are used to identify criminals. Skint back describes someone driving at a high rate of speed. Apin ass described someone who is driving at a high rate of speed and acting crazy. Rollin dirty is when someone is driving around with dope in their car.

Move Along; Nothing to See Here

I had to get used to strange answers to my questions; here's a sample:

"Hey, can I talk you real quick?"

"Who me?"

"Hey, where you going?"

"I'm just walking."

"You are under arrest."

"Why?"

"You got crack in your pocket."

"Ain't mine. These are my cousin's pants."

"Someone saw you over there, and they think you are slingin' crack."

"Ain't none of me."

We changed shifts every four weeks, and that was hard getting used to. We went from days to midnights to evenings. If you were on days and were switching to midnights you got off at 3:00 P.M. and had to come back at 11:00 P.M. if you didn't have the day off. If you were on evenings and switching to days, you got off at 11:00 P.M. and came back at 7:00 A.M. I had very little patience on those days.

Chapter 2

After completing the FTO program, I was assigned to the Third Precinct. My first night solo I left the precinct and looked at the passenger seat and realized I was ALONE. I thought, "Oh my, God—I'm the police!"

The officers on the squad I was assigned to were mostly veteran officers. One of my academy classmates, David Duke, joined me on the squad. David was retired military. I discovered he had issues in identifying with black people; he also didn't think before he spoke. We responded to a disturbance at a neighborhood bar in Toulminville. The people involved left the bar before we showed up. As we were walking back to our cruisers, he noticed a car in the parking lot and said, "This looks like a black person's car." The owner of the car happened to be standing within earshot, and he said, "What was that?" I thought, "This is great. You've started something now."

Most people would have quickly thought of something to say to smooth things over, since obviously, you just put both feet in your mouth. Not David. He repeated, "This looks like a black person's car." The owner said, "Why does this look like a black person's car?" David, totally oblivious to what he was saying said, "Well, the rims and tires, the fuzzy interior, the curb feelers, and everything else." I was dying. The owner must have realized David had no idea that he was being offensive, because he said, "You don't have any idea what your saying, do you?" I interrupted and said, "No, he doesn't." He said, "Someone is going to hurt him someday."

David and I answered another disturbance call in Toulminville a few days later. I had calmed everyone down except for one guy who was still venting, when David asked, "Hey, boy, what's the problem?" Everyone got quiet and stared at him; he didn't have a clue. The guy said, "Did you call me *boy*?" To keep from having to fight our way out of the neighborhood I said, "No. He was talking to me. He calls me

Move Along; Nothing to See Here

boy." Then I looked at David and said, "Why don't you meet me at the park in a minute." He said, "Okay" and left. The guy looked at me and said, "I think he was talking to me." I said, "No, he was talking to me." He walked away.

I met David and tried to explain why black men don't like to be called *boy*, especially by a white police officer. I'm not sure if he understood or not. David had some other issues that eventually led to him resigning. He was a super nice guy, but some people don't need to be police officers.

You learn that a complicated call is referred to as a *cluster*. A cluster sneaks up on you when you least expect it, and it usually starts out something so easy that you think you may not have to generate a report. The following is a classic example of a cluster. Dispatch sends me to a house in reference to a teenager falling off of a bicycle. I'm thinking, "Great—no paperwork on this one." I showed up and contacted the fifteen-year-old male. He had a three-inch wide band of road rash (abrasions) from above his left hip to his right shoulder. His left leg was mangled and he was in obvious pain. I asked him what happened, and he said, "I fell off my bicycle." I don't believe him. His aunt and a few other relatives came out as the ambulance stopped in front of the house.

I asked his aunt if she knew what happened. She pointed to a motorcycle leaning against the side of the house and said, "I think his dumbass was driving that thing. I told him to stay off of it. He was supposed to be going to Pookie's house." Motorcycle doesn't have a tag. I ran the VIN and discovered it's stolen. The EMT informed me they are going to take him to the hospital. He doesn't know what I've learned so far, and he definitely needs to get medical attention. I told him that I would see him at the hospital. His aunt informed me where Pookie lives and said she was going to try to contact her sister.

I turned onto Pookie's street. A guy standing in his front yard out by the street flagged me down and asked if I'm there for the crash. I asked, "What crash?" He was standing in his yard when he saw two guys on a motorcycle going pretty fast. The operator tried to go around the turn too fast and dumped the bike. The operator and passenger slid along the street several feet. The operator managed to get to his feet, got back on the bike, and left, with his buddy lying in the middle of the street. He told me that the passenger's nickname is Pookie, and he lives down the street. The witness called Pookie's momma and she came to get him and took him to the hospital.

I went to the hospital and discovered Pookie was there, and he was in even worse shape than his friend. I spoke with his mother, who wanted to beat the daylights out of Pookie's buddy. I learned that Pookie's friend was in a triage room on the other side of the E R. I decided not to share that bit of information with Pookie's mom because there's no need to complicate this further. Pookie's friend lied to me about his identity. After two names and three dates of birth I got his real name from him.

What started out as a simple kid falling off of his bicycle turned into receiving stolen property, leaving the scene of a crash with injuries, no driver's license, no motorcycle endorsement, and giving a false name to a law enforcement officer. Did I mention that Pookie's friend had an outstanding warrant?

Gang violence in the first six months of 1992 was almost out of control. There would be at least one reported drive-by shooting a week in the Third Precinct. The Gangster Disciples in Happy Hills, Bloods in Roger Williams, Folk and Crips in Orange Grove, and Crips in Toulminville didn't work and play well together. The housing projects in the First Precinct were in the same condition.

The Folk Nation is an alliance of street gangs based in the Chicago area that has since spread throughout the United States (specifically in the Midwest and the South) and into Canada. They are rivals to the People Nation. Within the Folk Nation alliance, there are many gangs that all have their own unique colors, hand signs, and organization. Many of these gangs have signed a charter to join the Folks alliance

Move Along; Nothing to See Here

formed on November 11, 1978 in an Illinois prison. Soon afterwards, the People Nation was formed to counter the Folks alliance.

Major gangs under the Folks alliance include Gangster Disciples, Black Disciples, Spanish Gangster Disciples, Maniac Latin Disciples, Imperial Gangsters, Spanish Cobras, La Raza Nation, Gangster Two Six, Latin Eagles, Simon City Royals, and insane gangster disciples, aka Satan Disciples.

The People Nation was formed in Chicago to counter the Folks alliance in 1978; the El Rukns now Black P. Stones, Vice Lords, and Latin Kings formed an alliance of their own, and titled it the People. Among initial members of the People were the Mickey Cobras then named the Cobra Stones, Latin Counts, Bishops, Insane Unknowns, Spanish Lords; the Gaylords and the South Side Popes, and later the Bloods subsequently joined the People.

The Black Gangster Disciple Nation was formed on Chicago's Southside in the late 1960s, by David Barksdale, leader of the Gonzanto Disciples, and Larry Hoover, leader of the Supreme Disciples. The two groups united to form the Black Gangster Disciple Nation. Gangster Disciples have been documented in the U.S. military and have been found on both U.S. and overseas bases. Graffiti characteristic of the Gangster Disciples has been reportedly seen in U.S. military bases in Iraq and Afghanistan.

Gangster Disciples follow a strict code and use symbols and hand signs to communicate alliances and rivalries. Some of the symbols and signs include a heart with six wings; an inverted numeral five is used to convey disrespect to any gang under the five-pointed star; a three-tined pitch fork aiming upward is a symbol for okay; and righting the Peoples Nation's inverted pyramid symbol conveys disrespect. A hand sign formed using fingers on both hands to resemble a six-pointed star, similar ot the Star of David is a reference and homage to David Barksdale. The points are supposed to represent life, love, loyalty, wisdom, knowledge, and understanding. Any of these can be incorporated in drawings, notes, hand signals, a private alphabet, or displayed in various forms on clothing and private or public property.

The Insane Gangster Disciples is a drug gang that began operating in northern areas of Birmingham, Alabama in the 1990s. The gang is affiliated with the Gangster Disciples and the national Folk Nation, and it has crews in several southern and midwestern states. The gang dresses mainly in black, favoring Oakland Raiders team gear. The letters *IGD* or the cipher 974 are seen in their graffiti tags.

The Bloods street gang formed at Centennial High School in Compton, California, and were originally known as Piru, which was taken from Piru Street in Compton. The Bloods were formed to protect members from the Crips. While the Bloods, or sets, are a smaller group than the Crips, they are very violent. At the time, Crips sets outnumbered Bloods sets by three to one. Traditionally, the Bloods street gangs have always worn red colors, using red bandannas or red rags; similar graffiti and graphic styles, emphasizing disrespect for Crips and their symbols. They have been known to wear brown, tan and rust or burnt orange colors to represent dried blood. They have also been known to wear pink, a variation of red.

In 1969 in Los Angeles, fifteen-year-old Raymond Washington organized a group in his neighborhood and started a gang called the Baby Avenues. The Baby Avenues wanted to copy a gang of older guys who had been involved in gang activity since 1964 and committed minor crimes for the Black Panthers of Los Angeles. This gang was called the Avenue Boys since they claimed their turf on Central Avenue in East Los Angeles. Raymond Washington, along with Stanley "Tookie" Williams and several other gang members from the Baby Avenues Gang were fascinated with the hype of the Black Panthers, and they wanted to develop the Baby Avenues gang into a larger force. The Baby Avenues Gang began using the name Avenues Crips since members lived on Central Avenue. Crip members would wear blue scarves (now called bandannas) around their necks or heads. The color blue became their representative color. Raymond Washington and his collection of idiots influenced other area gangs resulting in

Move Along; Nothing to See Here

the formation of many Crip sets. Some of these sets included Avalon Garden Crips, Eastside Crips, Inglewood Crips and Westside Crips. Two things Crips gangs have in common: they were violent and constantly expanded their turf.

Initiation into the Crips involves committing a crime in front of gang witnesses. The initiation process is called *locking-in.* Female members have the option to commit a crime or become *sexed-in*, which means having sex with several older members. Crips on the East Coast wear blue and clear beads or blue and white beads around their neck but mostly blue jeans and a white shirt. East Coast Crips affiliate with the Folk Nation gangs and have adopted the Folk Nation Symbols.

Gangs adopt sports teams and use the names to form their own meanings. The Crips and Folk wear University of Illinois clothing. The initials U and I together appear to be a pitchfork being thrown up. Folk use the Los Angeles Raiders. Raiders stands for ruthless ass insane disciples everywhere running shit.

Folks wear Duke University clothing. Duke stands for disciples using knowledge everyday. Crips wear Adidas. Adidas stands for all day I disrespect all slobs. Crips use the word Slobs when they talk about Bloods. Crips also like the Dallas Cowboys. Cowboys stands for Crips out west bangin' all you slobs. K-Swiss stands for kill slobs when I see slobs. Nike stands for niggas insane killing everybody. The Sacramento Kings clothing is worn and Kings stands for killin' innocent niggas gangsta style.

There are various styles of how a gang banger wears clothing. For instance, Crips wear one pant leg up and jewelry on the right side. Bandannas are tied around the right leg or arm, and girls use bandannas as a scrunchy. When wearing hats, the bill points to the right; there are numerous other variations of styles. The gangs in Mobile adopted all the tendencies of gangs in larger cities including the violent lifestyle.

Darrell McMann

The first murder I responded to was in Orange Grove on a nice quiet Sunday morning. A two-man ranger unit turned onto a street and found about 100 people standing in front of an apartment. They stopped to investigate and discovered someone had been shot; the crowd had been there for about ten minutes. The victim was on his knees at the front door; blood was running over the doorframe and onto the front porch.

The witnesses said two rival gang bangers showed up at the apartment. One had a sawed-off shotgun and the other had a handgun. The one with the handgun knocked on the front door and then backed down the steps and hid in front of the porch. When the victim opened the door, he started shooting at him, and the victim started shooting back. The guy with the shotgun came through the backdoor and shot the victim in the back of the head.

When I arrived I took a position in front of the apartment to keep people out of the crime scene. I also got to witness what we called *the show*. Within the crowd there were several types of people. There's the joker—he tells jokes and finds everything funny. There are the avengers—they walk up and down the street talking about how they are going to go get some, how they are going to pop some caps in the MF'er who killed their homeboy. The gawkers get as close as possible to the crime scene tape and lean as far as they can over the tape to see whatever they can possibly see. The curious walk through the crowd and ask everyone what happened. The visitors take advantage of the crowd of people to visit with people they haven't seen recently. The fallouts are women, and one of them will usually fall to the ground "unconscious" every few minutes.

While I was watching the show, the dispatcher called to inform me that a guy from an apartment across the street from the crime scene had called and said he was the victim of a robbery a few days before. This guy said that he was watching the suspect in front of the crime scene standing in the street. He described the suspect as a black male in his early twenties wearing a white T-shirt and blue jeans.

Move Along; Nothing to See Here

I looked around and saw at least fifty people who fit that description. I informed dispatch of that and told them to have him contact me and point the guy out. He refused to contact me which wasn't surprising.

One night in Orange Grove, paramedics responded to a 911 call of a person hurt on Dr. Martin Luther King. They arrived and found a large crowd on the scene. One of the people in the crowd pointed to an apartment and told them the person who was hurt was in the apartment. They called for an officer to meet them. They reached the individual who was hurt, but apparently he didn't want any help because he punched the paramedic who approached him. Two officers arrived and parked next to the rescue truck a block from the apartment. The officers found out where they were and entered the apartment just after the paramedic was punched. They arrested the guy without incident. They were walking him back to the cruiser when he noticed how many people were there. He began screaming and trying to pull away, which incited the crowd.

The officers quickly called for more units, and I was among the responding cavalry. When I got there an officer had parked the paddy wagon in the middle of MLK and opened the rear doors. The guy had calmed down and was about to get in when he decided to start more trouble. I was helping the other officers with the suspect until one of the officers told me to watch the crowd; I turned and saw five or six people creeping up on us. They stopped when I pulled out my baton, but they didn't back up. They got the guy in the wagon, and his dad ran up and tried to explain what happened. One of the officers told him to meet him at the city jail, and he could explain it to him there. The guy's dad started screaming and calling us crackers. My sergeant, Barney Frank drove up, saw the crowd, looked at us, and said, "Ya'll get the hell out of here!" He drove away immediately, and we left.

The guy's dad showed up at the jail with the same attitude. The officer tried to explain to him why his son was arrested. He didn't want to hear the explanation and became extremely disrespectful. The officer told him to calm down or leave. He rose so much cain the officer arrested him, too. His son had been riding with his girlfriend down

Darrell McMann

MLK, and he had been drinking and was being a turd. She told him to get out as she was turning into Orange Grove, and he opened the door and fell out on the pavement.

One quiet Sunday afternoon I was at the fire station outside Happy Hills watching a football game when we heard several gunshots. I notified dispatch as we ran outside to investigate. We heard people screaming and then twenty or thirty shots from an assault weapon. Barney ordered me to wait for backup, which wasn't too far away. While waiting, I heard another twenty or so more shots and more screaming. I got on the radio and advised that I had more shots fired. Just as my backup (five other units) arrived, we got a 911 call. We were all heading to the scene when I observed a black male running down Dr. Thomas Drive with an assault weapon. He heard us approaching and darted into the neighborhood outside Happy Hills and disappeared in the middle of the block. We set up a perimeter and spotted him quickly when he tried to get out of the neighborhood without his gun—he had tried to hide it in a tree. The fellow gang banger he was shooting at walked up to us shaking and with a terrified look on his face. I asked if he was hurt, and he said, "No. I can't believe it—he must have popped thirty or forty caps at me and didn't hit nothing." While I was talking to him, a bullet fell out of his pants leg unto the street. The bullet went through his pants below the groin and been stopped by excess material—baggy pants saved his future children.

Several people were drinking and playing dominos one afternoon in Happy Hills. Two guys got into an argument when they started talking about the size of their members. Someone in the crowd suggested they whip them out and whoever had the smallest member would have to buy the winner a beer. They unzipped and showed the world. The winner starts talking smack to the loser, and it quickly went downhill from there. The loser pulled out a knife with a curved blade and stabbed the winner in the abdomen.

When I arrived, the paramedics were already tending to the winner, and I noticed a beige bumpy blob lying on his chest. I asked the paramedic what it was, and he told me it was his intestine. The winner

Move Along; Nothing to See Here

noticed a crowd had gathered and stopped screaming. He looked at me and said, "I don't need no police. I will take care of it myself." Someone in the crowd yelled, "You ain't gonna do shit until they stuff your junk back in!" The crowd laughed at that, which just made the winner angrier.

One night someone from Happy Hills called and said a kid was walking down the street, and it looked like he had a gun. I found the kid—he was twelve-years-old. He didn't have a gun, but he did have a Disciples Book of Knowledge, and he was proud of it. It was a binder with about a hundred notebook pages depicting gang signs and everything else a prospective gang banger would need to know. He told me if I took it from him, he would get me. I told him I wasn't going take it from him, but I wanted to look at it. He said I could but that I couldn't tell anyone. I asked him how much of the book he had memorized and how long had he been looking at it. He told me he had memorized most of it in two weeks. I said, "You memorized this in two weeks? What kind of grades do you make in school?" He told me didn't go to school because "school ain't got nothin for me." He knew his life wasn't going to go anywhere, and he didn't care." He lived with his grandmother; his dad had been murdered, and his momma was in jail. He told me that "the Disciples are my family."

We were on the evening shift a week later and responded to a shots fired in the area call in Crichton. I was less than a block away and met another officer the middle of the block. I told him I hadn't seen or heard anything, and he hadn't either. We looked for another minute or two and then left the area.

About ten minutes later I was dispatched to a house on the same street for a person who had been shot. When I arrived, I noticed the door had been knocked off the hinges from the inside. Someone was trying to make it look like a home invasion. Another officer and I walked onto the porch. It was a shotgun house, so we could see all the way down the hallway to the kitchen. We could see a black male sitting in a chair in the kitchen with his back to us. We announced

Darrell McMann

our presence and slowly made our way to the kitchen; I kept my eye on the kitchen as my backup cleared the rooms as we made our way down the hallway. We reached the kitchen and discovered why the guy wasn't answering us. He had been shot in the head and was obviously dead. We also noticed a large pile of powder cocaine on the kitchen table and other items that are used to convert it to crack. The microwave oven was on—they were nuking crack. The deceased had a handgun is his waistband, and it was halfway out, so he probably recognized what was happening but was too slow on the draw.

I asked dispatch who had called about this, and they gave me the address next door. I walked out and found the neighbor standing in the yard. He asked if his niece was okay. I said, "Yeah, your niece is fine." I asked him who lived there. He said, "My niece and her boyfriend." I said, "Okay," and told him stay there, and I would be right back. I walked a few feet away and asked dispatch what the caller had said. They said he told them someone had been shot. I walked back over to the uncle/caller and asked if he had heard or seen anything suspicious. He said he didn't know, and when I asked him again who lived there, this time he said he wasn't sure. I didn't question him any further and turned him over to the first homicide detective that responded.

Homicide learned that the niece's boyfriend and the deceased had entered into a joint drug-dealing venture. They were in the kitchen converting the powder to rock when they began arguing. The boyfriend was convinced he was holding out on him and shot him. The niece ran next door to her uncle's house and told him to call 911 that someone was shooting. She ran back to the house.

The boyfriend told homicide that he opened the front door to leave when he noticed two police cruisers sitting in the street about two houses away; he closed the door and waited for us to leave. After we left, he decided to try and make it look like someone broke in and shot the guy. The niece ran back to her uncle's house and told him to call 911 again that someone had been shot.

Move Along; Nothing to See Here

Growing up, most men are taught to be respectful toward women and never raise your hand toward a woman. As a police officer, it's good idea to forget that while you are on duty. I responded three different times during a shift to a disturbance in Roger Williams involving a drunken female who was being a problem for everyone else. The first time, she told me she was sorry and would go back to her apartment. She was about six-foot-three and 250 pounds. The second time, she cussed me and went back to her apartment. I told her I would arrest her if I had to deal with her again.

When I arrived for the third call, she was waiting on me. She was telling everyone who would listen she was going to beat that cracker's ass when he comes back. I heard her when I got out of the car. I told her she was under arrest and, of course, she told me where I could put my handcuffs. I grabbed her left arm and attempted to force it behind her. She started turning in a circle. We went around three times, and she said loudly, "I can do this all night long," and I saw her form a fist with her right hand. I threw my hip into her and dumped her on the ground face first. She didn't realize that I was using her momentum to get her to the ground. When she hit the ground about thirty people laughed. I handcuffed her, and she spent the night in jail.

I began responding to the same house in Trinity Gardens frequently toward the end of every month. It would always be a family disturbance complaint. Every time I responded, I would find a rather larger black female standing in her front yard. She would say, "That little nigger crack head bastard did it again." He would smoke crack and aggravate her until she had enough and beat him with whatever she could grab. The first time I responded, she had beaten him with a frying pan. There was some awesome blood splatter on the wall. He always ran away before I got there. I asked her why they always fight at the end of the month. She said, "He gets a check for being crazy, and when the money gone, he gone!"

One day on the day shift I got a call to meet a female at the Circle K near Scott Paper Company on Telegraph Road. When I met her, she told me she needed to go to her husband's parents' house to

Darrell McMann

get her kids. She brought a friend with her for support. She told me her husband was in jail for beating her up. She had left her kids with his parents while she found another place to live; Ricky Weese and I escorted her.

When we arrived, I walked up the driveway to contact her father-in-law. He looked at me and then said to her, "You didn't need to bring the police here to get your kids." She told him she thought they were mad at her because their son was in jail. Before he could answer, the kids ran out of the house to her yelling "Mommy." While she and her friend were gathering the kids' clothing, her mother-in-law came home with two of her sisters. The mother-in-law told me that I could not let the kids go with her, and I asked her why. She told me because the state took them away from the mother and gave her temporary custody. I asked her if she had a caseworker's name, and she asked what that was. I told her that would be the person she would have been dealing with. She didn't know and didn't have a contact number, so I told her I couldn't stop her daughter-in-law from taking the kids. She began arguing with me, and I heard Ricky yelling, "HEY, HEY, HEY!" from in front of the house. The mother-in-law and I ran out to the street and found Ricky pulling one of the mother-in-law's sisters out of the back of a car as she was trying to take one of the kids out the car seat. Her other sister was trying to snatch the other child from the car. I stopped her and told the daughter-in-law to leave. After she left, the mother-in-law warned me she would have my job. I ignored her and left.

Two hours later Barney called dispatch to have Ricky and I meet him at the precinct. When we got there he said he needed both of us to write statements about what happened. Apparently the mother-in-law knew someone who knew the chief. Barney told us we gave the kids to wrong person. The female we released the children to wasn't their mother; the chief was pissed, and we were in trouble. I told him the father-in-law identified her as the children's mother, and the kids called her mommy. He said, "Just write the statements. It sounds like ya'll did the right thing."

Move Along; Nothing to See Here

We wrote our statements and gave them to Barney. Two days later Barney told us not to worry about anything. He said, "Ya'll ain't in hot water anymore. A couple of detectives from the juvenile division have taken your place in the hot water." The detectives had gotten a court order to remove the children from the custody of the person we gave them to—the actual mother. Apparently they gave the children to wrong person.

The children's father worked offshore and came home a couple of weeks early because he suspected his wife was cheating on him. When he got home he found his wife and her boyfriend loading everything from the house into a U-Haul truck. The husband and boyfriend had a brief fistfight. The wife and boyfriend jumped in the U-Haul and took off to get away from him. The husband gave chase, ran the U-Haul off the road, and shot the boyfriend after a brief struggle. The boyfriend was in the hospital and was expected to make a full recovery. I never heard anything else about it.

Chapter 3

On April 29, 1992, a Los Angeles jury acquitted four police officers in the beating of Rodney King. The verdicts were broadcast live, and as word spread quickly throughout the city, rioting erupted, lasting for three days.

I couldn't help but watch the news coverage. I remember watching Reginald Denny drive his eighteen-wheeler toward a group of guys standing in the street. I remember thinking "Don't stop. If you keep going, they will get out of the way." When he stopped, I said, "He's dead." The men pulled him from the truck and began to beat him; they continued to hit and kick him until he lost consciousness. I wondered if something similar would happen in Mobile.

Our squad worked the day shift in April 1992. Barney assigned me to a month on beat eighteen, which covered Happy Hills, Magazine, the northern part of the causeway, the port, the railroad terminal along the Mobile River, and neighborhoods east of Highway 43, outside of Chickasaw, Prichard, Saraland and Satsuma. Barney thought the beat had more abandoned vehicles than any other area, and he wanted me to placard every vehicle on the street that was in disrepair or that didn't have any tags. Either the owners moved the vehicles, or I had them towed. I'm not sure how many cars I tagged, but I was amazed at the number of vehicles I found. My squad changed shifts to midnights in May 1992

I was dispatched to an abandoned vehicle in the Magazine neighborhood within the first week we were on midnight shift. The caller, who refused to leave a name, told the dispatcher that the car was in disrepair and had been there for over a month. Otis Plotter, who was working the adjoining beat, knew I had spent April focused on abandoned vehicles and thought the call sounded suspicious so he advised dispatch he would back me up.

Move Along; Nothing to See Here

As we approached the location of the abandoned car, I observed several guys standing behind a car that was parked on the side of the street. The car's trunk was open, and the men were standing so that they had easy access to the trunk. They didn't plan it well because they were directly under a bright street light, and I could see them from a block and half away. What got my attention is that they were all staring straight at us and were standing close to the trunk. I made a quick decision and decided not to stop. I turned at the intersection and stopped about three blocks away. Otis pulled up next to me and said, "You just saved our lives. I think they were planning to ambush us."

I called Barney and explained what happened. He complimented me on my quick thinking. "Ya'll stay put. I'm sending a few units up there," Barney said. We waited for the additional units to arrive and then planned how best to approach the men. I walked to within a block of where I'd seen the men to see what was going on; they were gone, and so was the vehicle. Barney called dispatch and informed them to dispatch three units on all calls. He instructed everyone to wait for backup before arriving at a call.

While getting ready for work the evening of May 7th, I turned on my portable radio to get an idea of how busy the evening shift was. I heard dispatch trying to get officers to respond to several reports of shots fired in the Roger Williams housing project area. Dispatch was also trying to get officers to escort the fire department to several fires in the area. I thought, "Wow, they are hopping tonight." I turned my radio off and finished getting ready. I guess I was hoping it would calm down a little by the time we hit the street.

Chad Freeman and I were the first two officers from our squad to show up for work. Barney and Lieutenant Mark Rowe were standing at the back door of the precinct listening to the radio when we walked up. Before we could ask what was going on, Barney told us to get the keys to the paddy wagon (prisoner transport van) and go to the Soul House Lounge on St. Stephens Road. We were to transport witnesses to a shooting from the bar to headquarters, so that they could be

Darrell McMann

interviewed by homicide detectives. As he entered the building, Chad asked Barney what was going on, but Barney didn't hear him. Chad told me to get the keys. He didn't know what was happening and didn't like it. He went to his vehicle and grabbed his shotgun.

The Soul House Lounge was a hole-in-the-wall bar off St. Stephens Road; it had a small parking lot out front with spaces for about four or five cars. The area was so tight that some of the longer cars almost extended into the roadway. Earlier that evening a man and a woman were in the Soul House Lounge arguing, when he pulled a gun from his waistband and threatened to shoot her; someone in the bar called 911, and a two-man ranger unit that was just across the street in the Roger Williams responded..

The officers pulled into the only open space in the parking lot, which was directly in front of the front door, just as the suspect was backing out of the bar with the gun in his hand. The officers opened their doors and told the suspect that they were the police and to drop the gun. The suspect was very drunk and was focused on yelling threats at his girlfriend, so he didn't hear the officer's instructions. As he was arguing with his girlfriend he realized someone was yelling at him. He turned his head slightly and finally noticed the officers a few feet behind him. They told him again to drop the gun and lay on the ground. He started arguing with the officers and when he turned suddenly, both officers fired two or three rounds. The suspect died immediately. One round grazed the suspect and hit the female with whom he was arguing. She died about a week later.

There were several witnesses to the shooting in the bar, across the street, and a few walking down St. Stephens Road. They knew the shooting was justified and knew the female ran toward the door when the shooting started. Everything was fine until a rookie reporter from Channel 10 showed up.

The reporter walked over to two gang bangers from Roger Williams and asked them what happened. They told her two white cops shot an unarmed black man. She didn't bother to try and talk

Move Along; Nothing to See Here

to anyone else to corroborate the story or interview a police department spokesman. She went live on the 10:00 P.M. news and repeated what the two gang bangers had told her. It wasn't long before Roger Williams and a small section of Toulminville broke out into a period of civil disobedience.

When Chad and I showed up at the bar, I noticed David Garth standing on the west side of the parking lot wearing his riot helmet and holding his shotgun. I walked over to him, and he told me what happened. He whispered, "It's been quiet for a few minutes."

Chad walked back to the paddy wagon and told me the homicide detectives were going to bring out one witness at a time. While we waited we heard several gunshots from the east and west. They started bringing out the witnesses, and we heard more gun shots to the west and people screaming. We loaded up the witnesses and took them to headquarters. They were crammed in the paddy wagon like sardines. Several of them were drunk and were very displeased with the ride the police department had provided for them. We were in investigations at headquarters for about ten minutes when we found out an officer had been shot in Roger Williams. Chad asked the detectives if we could leave, but I don't think he waited for an answer.

Chad decided he would drive and took a curious route back to the area that I didn't question until I realized we were westbound on St. Stephens Road approaching Roger Williams. We could see the police on the south side of St. Stephens Road exchanging fire with people in Roger Williams. I thought Chad was going to stop and turn around, but he suddenly stomped on the gas pedal and yelled on the radio, "HOLD YOUR FIRE!" I was amazed that both sides quit shooting, but I guess everyone was amazed we were driving through—I know I was.

As we passed the entrance into Roger Williams, Chad slowed down. There was a vacant wooded lot on the west side of Roger Williams with an old ice cream stand near the road. People would use a path through the lot to go to the Circle K on the corner of St. Charles

Darrell McMann

and St. Stephens. Chad was busy looking behind us when I noticed someone standing on the east side of the ice cream stand. I had a hard time seeing him because it was now around 1:30 in the morning, and he was wearing dark clothing. I could see his left arm. It looked like it was straight down his side. I was about to say something to Chad when the guy brought his arm up, and I could see he had a long gun in his hand. We were right on top of him when he fired a shot. I ducked, some of the pellets struck my door post.

Chad went into a power slide in the parking lot of the Circle K and grabbed me to see if I was okay. I told him I was, but I added sarcastically that he had just broken my neck. Despite our situation, that made us both laugh. He got on the radio and reported that we had just been shot at. We were told to stay at the Circle K to protect it. I looked over and noticed that every window was broken out and the only thing left in the store was a bottle of Sprite and a pack of Twizzlers. Lt. Rod Webb and Sgt. Jeff Sweat came to check on us and filled us in on everything that was happening. They told us to stay at the Circle K and then left. Chad decided that we would go to the east side of the Circle K, so we could watch for anyone coming down St. Charles and from one of the trails through the vacant lot.

Chad and I crouched down behind some bushes to conceal ourselves, so we could see if anyone was coming through the vacant lot or down St. Charles. We were talking quietly while watching for whatever might come our way. I looked at him and said, "You know, this might be a good time to decide if I really want to do this job." I had been a solo officer for only three months. I could see him glaring at me; I knew he was trying to figure out if I was going to leave him there if things got chaotic. We had never worked a call together. He was about to say something when I told him not to move. A police cruiser was slowly easing down St. Charles with both back doors open. The front passenger and both officers in the back seat had long guns. When they turned on St. Stephens, I looked at Chad and said, "Don't worry I ain't going anywhere." He said, "That's good. I would hate to have to shoot you in the head." We laughed.

Move Along; Nothing to See Here

While crouching in the bushes, we could hear the shootout continuing east of us along St. Stephens Road and heard a couple of shots coming from the wooded area of the vacant lot. A few minutes later, we saw someone standing in a clearing on the lot and shooting at the officers across the street; the individual then began looking in our direction. Chad said, "Get ready, if he gets closer, were going to go get him." He kept getting closer and would shoot every few minutes. We noticed his attention was more focused on the officers down the street. Chad said, "On three we go." He was going left, and I was going right, but when we stood up to go, I noticed a group of ten or twelve people emerge from the woods closer to St. Stephens. I grabbed his arm and pointed down the street. We decided to see what they were going to do.

They noticed the paddy wagon in the parking lot of the Circle K and stood quietly for a few seconds assessing the situation. One of them crept up to it and discovered it was empty. A couple of them started throwing rocks and bricks at it until they lost interest. Chad got on the radio and quietly asked for additional officers. One of them started walking sideways down St. Charles toward us talking trash to no one in particular. He got within three feet of me and looked right at me but didn't realize anyone was there until he heard our radios. I jumped up and put my gun three inches from his forehead and ordered him to the ground. He yelled, "POLICE" and took off running toward his buddies; they were about to run when they noticed there were only two of us. They decided to stand and fight, and started talking about what they going to do to us. They were about one hundred feet from us, and we could see that a couple of them had something in their hands. Chad had his shotgun, and I had a 9MM. Chad yelled, "WE AIN'T GOING ANYWHERE!" One of them raised their arm toward us, and we started shooting.

When I started shooting everything slowed down, and my peripheral vision vanished—I was totally focused on what was directly in front of me. I remember thinking, "I can't believe I'm actually shooting at someone." My shots sounded muffled and echoed like one of those old western movies. I'm not sure if anyone in the crowd returned fire

Darrell McMann

because they were falling over each other trying to run back toward the projects. I'm not sure if we shot anyone or not, but I saw a couple of guys trying to help their friends get out of the area.

Chad and I had advanced to the ice cream stand by the time help arrived. He turned to me and said, "You see the two large trees? If we get to them, we can clear this lot out." I nodded and stepped out from behind the stand. I took one step and was hit in the chest. My breath had been knocked out me, and I thought for a minute I had been shot. Lt. Webb ran up, grabbed me, and got me behind the stand. He asked if I was okay, and I said, "I think so." He said, "Someone threw a concrete block at you." I heard someone laughing and looked around the side of the stand and saw a guy behind a tree pointing at me. I yelled, "You throw like a girl, jackass. You wanna try again?" He yelled a few things and ran back into Roger Williams through the vacant lot.

About an hour later, after the firefight ended, Chad and I were sent a few blocks over to assist a team that was going into Roger Williams to rescue a group of officers who had been pinned down for several hours behind a wall with several prisoners on Brazier Drive. Chad and I would be in the paddy wagon accompanied by eight officers on foot—four on each side of us. We were to make our way slowly down the street, shooting out the streetlights as we went to make it harder for the rioters to see and shoot an officer. Chad found a shotgun for me before we left. As we eased down the street, shooting out the streetlights, I couldn't help but think, "Hey, is this pretty cool." We got the prisoners and the officers out with no problems. Even the prisoners seemed happy to see us. The sun came up about an hour later, and everything was quiet.

We were ordered to come in at 7:00 P.M. and work twelve-hour shifts until further notice. That night I was assigned to Roger Williams with thirteen other officers in seven two-man cars. We parked at different locations, so we would be visible. The SWAT team silently walked through and contacted several people who were lurking in the shadows. It seemed like no one ventured away from his apartment that night. By then, most people had found out what really

Move Along; Nothing to See Here

happened at the bar, but there were a few people who wanted to stir things up anyway.

The next night I was solo in Orange Grove. Nothing had happened there yet, but the department assigned several units there for the night. At about 2:30 A.M., I noticed a lawn mower was on fire underneath a back porch. We didn't have fire extinguishers, so I had dispatch notify the fire department. I asked the dispatcher to have the fire department to send only one truck and to respond without lights or siren. She informed me it was their policy that they respond with the apparatus they thought they would need. I politely told her I understood that, but I didn't want to wake anyone up. I didn't want to give anyone any reason to get something started. I was sure that they would understand. She again told me it was their policy to respond with lights and siren, and to send whatever apparatus they thought they would need. A lieutenant broke into our exchange over the radio and told her to do as I asked.

The fire department sent one truck, and it arrived without lights flashing or siren blaring; the fire was out within a minute. The crew told me thanks, and they left. I looked back and noticed a guy at the back door of the apartment. I walked over and told him his lawn mower had been on fire, but everything was okay now. He said, "Yeah, thanks," and closed the door. I thought, "Yeah, you are welcome," shrugged, and walked back to my cruiser.

The next morning at around 2:00 A.M. a two-man unit noticed a male running east on Springhill Avenue in Crichton. They pulled up next to him and noticed that he was wearing a jogging suit. The officers also noticed he had drinking straws in both nostrils and in both ears. He looked at them and didn't break stride. They asked him why he had straws in his ears and his nose, and he said, "Because I can." Using their computer, they sent a message to another unit in the area. The second unit pulled alongside the first unit, and those officers told them to look at the jogger. The second unit pulled alongside the jogger and asked the same question. He gave the same response.

Darrell McMann

My partner and I had breakfast at the Waffle House at Dauphin Street and I65. We were headed back to Toulminville when we noticed four police cars following someone who was running on Springhill. We pulled up next to one of the cruisers and asked what was going on. They told us to check out the jogger. We pulled alongside him, and it was the guy with the straws. When my partner asked what was up with the straws, he looked at us and said, "Put them there because I could." He continued running north on Stanton Road. The first unit followed him until he crossed into Prichard.

We worked twelve-hour shifts for the rest of the week but nothing else happened. The officer who was shot was okay; he was shot in the arm but had no lasting physical effects. Several people went to local hospitals and claimed to have been shot by the police. They didn't know who shot them and refused to talk to investigators. I heard that the FBI was notified, but I was never interviewed and to my knowledge, no one else was.

A few months after the brief period of civil unrest, an officer from another squad at the precinct asked me if I was the officer that got hit in the chest with the concrete block. When I told him that I was, he said, "I arrested a guy this morning for burglary. While I was interviewing him, he asked me if my chest still hurt. I asked him what he was talking about. He told me he had hit me in the chest with a concrete block during the riot. I remembered what happened to you, so I told him that it wasn't me he'd hit, but I would give his name to the officer he threw the block at. Thanks for the confession. What an idiot."

We laughed about it, and he gave me the name of the suspect. I thought about it and decided I wouldn't do anything because it only knocked the wind out of me and the guy was looking at a couple of years already. I figured I would eventually run into him again somewhere.

Kim and I were married on September 19, 1992. I moved in with her in the apartment she was renting after our honeymoon.

Move Along; Nothing to See Here

Kim started talking about buying some land and buying a trailer. I wasn't very excited about that, but I decided I would look. They were nicer than I thought, so I decided it would be a good idea. We eventually found a trailer we liked and found a nice trailer park in Grand Bay.

Chapter 4

I learned when I returned from the honeymoon that I was being transferred to another squad in the Third Precinct, which was the squad I wanted to be on when I completed the FTO program. I had spoken with Sgt. John Sweet during the last week of FTO about being assigned to the squad, but there weren't any openings. Sgt. Sweat asked if I would like a permanent beat. I said, "Sure, but what about the rest of the squad?" He said, "It's okay because no one wants seventeen on a permanent basis." Beat seventeen encompassed the west end of Martin Luther King, Roger Williams, the west end of the Bottoms, and the north end of Toulminville.

My beat partner was Corporal Ron Adams. Ron quickly became my mentor though I didn't follow his example all the time. I learned from Ron how to *police*. I had been solo for about six months when I transferred and had worked with some very good officers, but they weren't very proactive. They would take the arrests that came their way but didn't really go looking for stuff to get into.

The first call I answered with Ron was a family disturbance in Orange Grove. One of the residents was hosting a family reunion when a couple of the guests began arguing. We went into the apartment and found about dozen people screaming at each other. Ron walked over to a table where a buffet was set up. He picked up a plate and started filling it. Everyone, including me, stared at him in disbelief. They quit arguing after a few minutes and watched him eat as he leaned against the wall. He asked who the host was, and then asked that person to tell him what the problem was. Ron worked out the issues and finished his meal. On the way out, he told them thanks for the food and hoped the rest of their visit would be good. He looked at me and said, "They were just worked up, give them a few minutes, and they will calm down." He got in his cruiser and left.

Move Along; Nothing to See Here

Ron noticed that I was working a major crack house in the Bottoms on Patton Avenue, which was a dead end. He told me he was happy to have someone working next to him who wanted to work. He introduced me to the family members in the house; he had arrested all of them sometime during their lives. He looked across the street and asked me if I had seen a black male standing in front of the house close to the street. I told him I had and that I'd noticed he walked in the house when he noticed I was coming down the street. He told me his first name is George, he is a convicted felon, and according to a confidential informant or CI, always carries a gun. He told me I would have to sneak up on him to get him. He told me to get in my cruiser and follow him because he wanted to introduce me to some people.

We drove several blocks and parked in front of a house. He told me the house had been abandoned and that a guy had taken it over and turned it into a Skins house. We walked in the house, and there were card games set up in every room. We heard a thump on the floor in the living room over the music and walked over to the card table. Ron picked up a 9MM off the floor and asked if it belonged to anyone. Everyone ignored him, and he said, "Yeah, I didn't think so." He introduced me to several people who really weren't interested in meeting me. Ron would share the history of each individual with me. They all seemed to genuinely trust him even though he had arrested them all.

We walked outside, and two black females approached us. One of them looked at Ron and said, "Hey, Adams, who is this little cracker honkey MF'er?" He laughed and told her this is officer McMann. She told me Ron went where no other white cop would and everyone respected him. She looked at Ron and asked if this little cracker was his new partner. He told her I was. She said, "Well hell, MF'er, you is now Baby Adams." Everyone in the neighborhood called me Baby Adams from that point on.

Sgt. Sweat had me come to the office after roll call one day. He asked me if I would be interested in becoming a FTO, and I told him I hadn't ever thought about it. "I've been an officer an officer for about 10 months, don't I need more experience?" I asked. He told me I was

Darrell McMann

doing a great job, and they had confidence in me; I told him I would give it a shot. He told me when I came back from my off days I would be getting a trainee. His current FTO, Marty Grove, worked Toulminville and was about to pull his hair out. Sgt. Sweat thought the rookie might be scared of black people, and Marty didn't know how to help him; he thought that since I stayed in the neighborhood and talked to people, I might be able to help him.

I met Tony when we came back from our off days. I had seen him on calls with Marty but didn't pay much attention to what he was doing. I told him to drive and where to go. We drove through Roger Williams, and we didn't see anyone because he went through so fast. I told him to go to the Bottoms. He went about fifty mph between stop signs for several blocks. It was a nice warm day, so there were people walking; I told him to stop the car. I asked him what his problem was, and he just looked at me. I told him to roll his window down and look around. He did. "You are driving fifty miles per hour between stop signs, dodging pedestrians—what's the problem," I said. He spread his arms and said, "THIS!"

Tony came from a college campus police department. He was Italian and about six-feet-eight with a thick build. I asked him if black people gave him the heebie-jeebies. He said, "I've never been in a neighborhood like this." I told him 99 percent of the people in this neighborhood are good people. They just happen to be poor and black. He said, "They look at me strange." I told him they were looking at you to try to see what you are about. If you work this neighborhood a lot, you will gain a reputation. Most people don't trust the police department but do trust individual officers. I had him get out of the car and talk to people over the next few weeks. I told him he needed to be more open. People share more information if you let them talk, and they think you are listening. He was coming around by the time he left me after four weeks.

The last night he worked with me was a Sunday night. He made a traffic stop on MLK. I was standing outside our cruiser while he was writing a traffic citation. Two teenagers were walking down a side

Move Along; Nothing to See Here

street to the east of us talking loudly. I heard one of them say we better be quiet there's five oh . The second kid looked over and said "F THE POLICE!" I thought, "Yeah, whatever."

They purposely walked toward us and walked between the cruiser and the car we stopped. Tony was having the driver sign the citation; the second kid looked at me and gave me a go-to-hell look as they walked across MLK. He looked back again and said, "F THE POLICE!" and continued walked east. I watched them as they turned south down a side street two blocks away. As I lost sight of them, dispatch called Ron and gave him a call two blocks from where we were. A witness observed two black male juveniles attempt to break into a car. The witness gave a description of the two kids I had just seen. I told Ron they just walked by us and told him the street where I'd last seen them walking.

Tony got back in the car, and I told him let's go. He asked, "What's up?" I asked him if he heard the call on the radio. He said, "No." I asked if he heard me on the radio. He said, "No." I said, "I hope I never get shot because you wouldn't hear it. NOW LET'S GO!"

We turned down the street, and I saw them crossing through the next intersection. I said, "There they are." He passed them. I yelled, "STOP!" He slammed on the brakes. I bailed out and said, "Don't just sit there, do something!" He got out and stood there. The respectful kid walked up to me and put his hands on the trunk when I asked him to. The rude kid froze. I said to Tony, "Would you PLEASE do something other than stand there like a DORK!" He asked what he should do, and I said, "Get HIM!" By now, Tony was boiling; he looked at the kid and in his best baritone voice yelled, "COME HERE!" The kid dropped to his knees in the middle of the street and started screaming over and over, "DON'T KILL ME!!"

Tony froze, too, but didn't fall to his knees and scream. I walked over and told the kid to stand up. I escorted him over to the cruiser. I felt his chest—his heart was about to beat a hole out of his chest. We discovered the witness observed one of the kids bend down next to

Darrell McMann

the car to tie his shoe and couldn't see what he was doing. The car had a broken window, but the caller only noticed it after the boys walked away.

We happened to be in front of the respectful kid's house and talked to his mother about what happened. She thanked me and told me she had told her son to stay away from his new friend. We took the rude kid home; he lived with his grandmother. She asked me where he had been. She said, "He told me he was going to get a haircut at the barber shop." I told her he couldn't get a haircut at nine o'clock on a Sunday night. I told her about the language I heard him use and that Tony scared the daylights out of him. She laughed and said, "Well, maybe that will get something through his thick head."

Most rookie officers know two speeds the first time they get behind the wheel of a cruiser—as fast as you can go and stop. I have never enjoyed driving fast because there are too many things that happen, and they are all bad. Driving in general usually drove me nuts when I had a trainee. I learned to tell them to drive just like it was their own personal vehicle. Rookies, including myself, would be overcome with the thought of, "I can't believe I'm driving a police car," and not pay attention to how fast they were driving. The first time you drive with the lights and siren going is nerve racking, especially for the FTO. The first instinct for a rookie is to drive as fast as possible and assume people hear and see you. Even though the lights and siren are going, you still have to stop at red lights and stop signs. You are requesting people give you the right of way. You have to remember you are out driving the siren, and some people won't realize your there until you are directly behind them. You have to watch for people and then give them a second or two to move over. It's best to pass on the left side, to avoid the other drivers' blind spots, and to try to keep from switching lanes so people will know how to react. So while you are driving at high speeds, with your lights and siren running and paying attention to everyone else around you, you also have to listen to the police radio, the stereo is more than likely too loud, the laptop is a distraction, you're thinking about your tactics, and running scenarios through your head to get yourself ready for what you may find when

Move Along; Nothing to See Here

you arrive at the scene. If you can't multitask then you need to go find something else to do.

I got a call to meet a female in Orange Grove in reference to a theft. I contacted her, and she told me her food stamps had been stolen. I asked where they were stolen from, and she didn't answer. I asked her what happened to them, and she looked up at a second floor apartment. I could hear several women's voices coming from the apartment. I said, "Did one of them take your food stamps." She said, "One of them has them, but they didn't take them." I asked her what happened. She said, "I lost them gambling while playing cards."

I looked at her and said, "Let's go." When we walked into the apartment, it became incredibly silent. I asked if everyone was here that has been involved in the card game. One of the ladies nodded yes. I told them they would never understand how incredibly stupid and sorry they were for gambling with their food stamps. I said, "I can't believe any of you would be pathetic enough to take food out of a child's mouth because of his mother's stupidity. Everyone in this apartment needs to have the exact amount of food stamps she came in here with." Food stamps were shuffled until each woman had hers. Then I said, "Before anyone leaves, I need your name, social security number, date of birth, and your address. I am going to turn over your information to the government. All of you will be fined one thousand dollars, get six months in jail, and lose your food stamp eligibility for three years. If you refuse or give me false information, I will arrest you now." They all complied. I was bluffing of course; I didn't want to punish a child for his mother's stupidity. I would see them every once in a while, and they would ask what was going on. I told them it's the federal government, they are slow but don't worry, they will get around to investigating it soon.

A few days later I responded to a disturbance in Happy Hills. When I arrived I saw one guy surrounded by four women. Each one of them was holding at least one baby. They were all very displeased with him. One lady was telling him he wasn't getting anymore than he was already getting. The ladies wouldn't speak to me, so I took him off to

Darrell McMann

the side. He told me he had talked these four women into allowing him to father their children without having to take any responsibility. Each woman had three kids and two of them were pregnant. He was getting a cut of each check the women got for their kids. He told me he'd found a decent woman who he thought was also pregnant by him. He wanted more money, so he could buy a house when he gets married to the new girl. I told him he was an incredibly stupid person. They could simply refuse to give him any money and where would he be then? He said he would get tested. I told him he was a genius and asked if he realized just how expensive the test was and that he would have to pay for each paternity test. He had no idea. Then I asked if he knew for sure he was the father of all the children. He said not really. I told him if the test proved he was the father, he would have to pay child support. He said he hadn't thought about that. I asked him if he had a signed contract detailing the specifics of the agreement he made between the women and himself. He said no they had just talked about it. I told him he would end up in court trying to prove they knowingly were committing fraud. The end result would be him spending a long time in federal prison. Again, he didn't have a clue about the ramifications of his actions.

The girls had walked over close enough to hear our conversation and were nodding eagerly in agreement. I said, "I wouldn't be happy if I were any of you. Ya'll could end up in prison, too. I'm so disgusted that I don't know what to say. Ya'll should be nominated for worse parents of the year. Congratulations, why don't ya'll go ahead and take your kids to the county jail and get their names entered in the system and get them fitted for jumpsuits."

The guy looked at me and told me he would leave things as they were and walked away. The women stood there for a minute; one of them asked me if she should continue dealing with him. I told her to figure it out for herself, and I left.

One Friday afternoon I responded to a disturbance in Orange Grove. A woman had found out her boyfriend was cheating on her. She told him she wanted to break up, but he didn't want to. When I

Move Along; Nothing to See Here

got there he was standing in front of the apartment yelling and cursing. I told him he needed to chill out. He told me where I could go and started screaming and cursing again; I arrested him. He got out of jail about three hours later and went back to his girlfriend's apartment. She called again because he was outside screaming and cursing again. When I arrived, I said, "You need to chill, or you're going back to jail." He said, "Whatever. Let's go," and then he started cursing again. He went to jail again.

I worked overtime on the midnight shift that night, and the first call was to that same apartment. When I got there, he was in the apartment. He had actually kicked the front door open and punched her several times. He saw me and said, "Put 'em on me cracker. I will be out soon anyway." I cuffed him and said, "You won't be out till Monday, genius." He asked why. I said, "You broke down the door and beat on her. I'm charging you with burglary and a felony assault. It's domestic violence, so you won't see a judge until Monday morning. Got anything else to say?" He didn't have anything to say.

A couple of days later, I was stopped at a four-way stop in an intersection in the Bottoms. I was thinking about where I wanted to go when a car heading the opposite direction stopped also. I heard someone yelling in the car, and the driver started honking the horn. The driver eased through the intersection and slowly drove by me. He was laughing maniacally and honking the horn. He had two passengers in the car who looked terrified. I yelled, "What's your problem," but he kept laughing and drove away. I turned around and activated my lights, but he kept going. He got on MLK and headed toward Orange Grove. He turned into Orange Grove and drove all over the projects with me behind him. His two passengers were yelling at him and kept looking back at me. He came back out onto MLK and headed back toward Roger Williams, honking his horn the whole time.

We drove back through the Bottoms for a few minutes and back onto MLK. He stopped briefly and his passengers jumped out. I pulled up next to them, and they both yelled, "He's crazy!" It wasn't too hard to catch back up to him because he never got over twenty-five miles per hour. I was calling the chase on the radio and waiting for backup, but it took a while. We were shorthanded, and I was the only officer in service in the precinct at the time.

He drove back into Orange Grove and sped up to around forty miles per hour. The first unit to reach the area was able to get parallel to him and blocked the intersection that we were approaching. The guy stopped the car and lay across the front seat. I was about to open the passenger door when he used his big toe to push the lock closed. His brother ran up as I was about to break out the window with my baton. He told me he was his brother and that he was crazy and hadn't taken his medication today. He asked me if he could try and talk him out of the car. I told him to go ahead. He talked to him through the window for a few minutes, and he unlocked the door. His sister walked up with a glass of water and a pill bottle.

Lt. Webb asked me what I was going to do. I thought for a second and asked if it was okay if we made believe it never happened. He said, "Sounds like a plan," and he patted me on the shoulder and left.

As a police officer, one sense you learn to trust is your sense of smell. I responded to several houses you could smell from the street. It's difficult for me to describe. Basically it's a mixture of urine, rotting trash, and feces mixed together. When you walk in a house and gag, it's time to leave. If I could smell it from the street, I didn't go in, I would have them come out. You get foul odor calls, and you cringe because you know you are going to find someone who has been dead for a while.

You also learn not lean against walls and doorframes because roaches would hitch a ride on you. I would hate to walk in a dark house and hear crunching everywhere I stepped. I would try to leave quickly because I didn't want to know how many roaches were running around. I couldn't believe the number of people who didn't wash their dishes. I'd enter a house or apartment and there would be a pile of dishes in the sink and leftover food lying around in the kitchen. That mess would attract a mixture of roaches and water bugs. I walked

Move Along; Nothing to See Here

into a few houses where bugs were trapped in drinks that had been spilled on the floor or counter.

One night Greg Mass and I responded to a domestic disturbance in Orange Grove. The lady's husband had grabbed her neck and tried to choke her, leaving hand prints on her neck. He broke out several windows and left. She said he had been smoking crack all day. She wanted him arrested, so I got all the information I needed and left to write a report. The suspect came back to the house ten minutes later, so we were called back. He broke out several more windows and left before we could get there. She gave us a description of his truck. Greg left to look for the truck. I told her I was going to go around the corner and wait to see if he came back; I was gone two minutes when she called again.

When I pulled into the parking lot, I could see him standing behind the apartment with something in his hand. I drew my gun and told him to drop whatever he had in his hand. He took a few steps toward me, and I yelled, "I will shoot you!" He stopped and threw down what turned out to be a broom handle. He yelled, "I'm leaving!" and snatched his keys out of his pocket and walked toward the truck. He opened the door, and I realized he wasn't getting in—he was reaching for something. I grabbed the back of his shirt and yanked him out. He stumbled back a few steps and faced off with me. He threw a punch, which I ducked; I gave him a solid right uppercut and a left to the abdomen. It didn't have any effect on him. He threw another punch that grazed my chin as I was moving to my right. He ducked and then stood up quickly, and I hit him with a forearm to the chin, which knocked him off balance. I shoved him against the truck and managed to get a chicken-wing hold on him. I felt his shoulder pop, but he kept fighting. I kneed him in the groin from behind but that didn't seem to bother him either. I looked toward the apartment and could see his wife standing in the apartment looking through a broken window pleading with me not to shoot him. Greg ran up a few seconds later, and we put him on the ground and cuffed him. I asked Greg to look in the truck while I put him in my cruiser. Greg walked over to me a few minutes later. "This is what he was trying to get,"

Darrell McMann

Greg said as he showed me a large butcher knife that had been under the front seat.

Before I left, I walked over to talk the wife. She told me thanks and that she was glad I didn't shoot him. As I was leaving, I was approached by two Crips. One of them said they had watched the whole thing and asked if I was Baby Adams. I told him that's what I'm called. He said, "I told my nigga we gotta help Baby Adams if he gets in trouble, but you handled it. I woulda capped the nigga." I said, "Yeah, okay, thanks."

Two nights later I was stopped at a red light on Martin Luther King when I noticed a blue truck across the intersection also stopped at the light. I could see two people sitting close together in the front seat; I recognized the truck. When the light changed, I saw the wife practically sitting in her husband's lap. The three of us looked at each other. I wanted to say, "Don't you remember that less than a day and a half ago he was trying to kill you?"

One morning around 2:00 a.m., I met Jerry Fanch, aka JoJo, age twelve. JoJo was walking up Martin Luther King with several other kids his age, and they all had baseball bats. I stopped to see what was going on. JoJo told me they were going to get rid of all the prostitutes on the avenue. I told him he was going about it the wrong way and called all their parents to come pick them up.

Ron told me that JoJo was the head poobah of a group of seven or eight boys that called themselves the Bottom Boys. He told me that JoJo loved starting fires and to go by JoJo's house and look at all the black marks in the street. Jo Jo's little gang hung out on the steps of a neighborhood church—JoJo took the top step and his fellow gangsters were seated from top to bottom according to their rank. They were usually involved in some mischief somewhere close by.

One night they kept me pretty busy; I found them in front of a vacant house, so I had them all assume the position along the front of the house and searched them; several neighbors were watching us.

Move Along; Nothing to See Here

One of them was feeling a little chippy and told me he his parents pay taxes that pay my salary. I asked him what his dad did for a living and learned that he was in jail. I asked what his mom did for a living. He told me she stayed at home and got a check. I told him that his daddy didn't pay taxes in jail, and I was paying for his daddy to sit in jail and eat for free and watch the cable TV I was also paying for. I told him my money went to his momma's check, so he could thank me for having a big screen TV, food to eat, and a place to live. I suggested that if he wanted a refund for the taxes that his momma pays, he should come over here. We walked out to the street, and I unscrewed the cap from one of the valve stems on one of the tires and handed it to him. "Here you go—this should cover it," I said. He got mad but didn't say anything; the neighbors thought it was hilarious.

Chapter 5

Ricky Weese approached me in March 1993 about becoming his partner in the Special Operations Jaguar Unit. The Jaguar Unit drove low-profile marked cars in uniform. The teams consisted of a black and a white officer or what we called *salt and pepper teams*. The idea was to cut down on biased complaints. At the time there was one Jaguar unit assigned to each precinct and your supervisor was whoever happened to be working.

I had worked with Ricky on the first squad I was assigned to and enjoyed working with him, so I transferred. We were an odd couple. He was black, six-foot-five, about 265 pounds, and had grown up in the inner city in Birmingham. I was white, five-foot-eight, about 200 pounds, and had grown up in the country. We obviously had different perspectives.

The first night we worked together, we rolled up on a disturbance in Toulminville. We quickly separated everyone involved. It was just an argument, so we had everyone go their own way. I thought it was over with until one of the guys told Ricky he was an Uncle Tom. The guy looked at me and told me to take my nigger home. He looked back at Ricky and told him he would whip his ass if he didn't have a gun and badge on, and then he said, "You ain't nothin without it."

Ricky said, "OH, YEAH?" He said to me, "Hold this." He handed me his badge and then took off his gun belt and handed it to me. We all stood there in disbelief, and the mouth took off running. Ricky took off after him yelling, "WHERE YOU GOING?" He chased him for a block and turned around. He told me he would take care of him later. I didn't know what to think.

The next night we were driving slowly down Green Street in Magazine. We pulled up next to a guy standing in the middle of the street drinking out of a whiskey bottle. Ricky told him to get in his yard. The guy ignored Ricky and took a big gulp. Ricky got out of the car and approached him; I put the car in park. As I was getting out Ricky knocked him out in the middle of the street with an open-hand slap. I walked over to him and thought he had killed him at first. Several people started coming out of their yards to confront us. I handled them while Ricky dragged the guy to our cruiser. The guy came to while I was dealing with the crowd. A couple of them said they knew I didn't see it because I was still in the car. They said Weese is a bad cop, and they wanted to speak to a supervisor. I gave them a phone number, and we left.

When we left the jail, Ricky asked me if I was wondering what I had gotten myself into. He apologized and told me he didn't expect me to lie for him if we found ourselves in a situation. He told me he grew up in a rough neighborhood, and it pissed him off to hear the same excuses that he heard back then. He shared with me that he was gang banger until midway through the tenth grade. He told me he walked up behind a man on the street and hit him in the back of the head with a board, knocking him out. He rolled him over to check his pockets and realized it was his girlfriend's father. He decided to spend more time playing sports after that incident. He told me he was taught that white people steal your knowledge. He told me he didn't shake that idea until he enlisted in the navy. Ricky and I had many conversations about race, perceptions, and reality. We were driving down MLK one afternoon when he asked, "Do you see that?" I asked, "What?" He said, "The power poles. Every one of them is leaning." I looked for a few minutes and told him he was right. Then he asked me if I ever counted the churches and chicken places. "No, are there a lot?" I asked. He glared at me and said, "Yes, why do you think that is?" I said, "Because black people like to go to church and enjoy chicken?" He smiled and nodded. "The poles are crooked because Alabama Power doesn't think anyone will notice all the power poles are crooked," I said. He nodded. I asked him why black people walked in the middle of the street when there is a perfectly good sidewalk a few feet away. He said, "Because we can."

Several veteran white officers approached me when it was announced that Ricky and I would be partners. They were concerned about me because they felt Ricky was an "extremist" and was trouble. I listened to what they had to say and went about my business. I told him later what I had been told. It kind of pissed him off, but he appreciated me telling him. He said, "It's nineteen ninety-three, and a black man can't voice his opinion." I told him not let it bother him.

Morale in 1993 was very low at the police department. There had been several scandals involving the chief, and there were rumors of other issues involving him. The city decided to have every function of the department evaluated from top to bottom. The Police Executive Research Forum or PERF was contacted. Every member of the department was told he might be contacted by a PERF representative, and we were to cooperate fully. One veteran officer quipped that he had been screwed many times by the department but never PERF'D.

Ricky and I were called in to be interviewed separately. I was asked if I thought the black fingerless gloves some officers wore were intimidating to black people. I said, "I don't know. I don't wear gloves, and I'm not black. I had never heard anyone say anything about it." He asked me if the department was biased toward black or white officers. I told him it depended on the individual. You can't just say an organization as a whole is racist. Apparently I didn't say what he wanted to hear, and he told me he didn't have any further questions for me. Ricky on the other hand talked for about forty-five minutes. He told me that when he was finished, he told the guy he wasn't sure why he talked to him because nothing is going to change.

Later that night we rolled up on a fight in Orange Grove. I thought it was strange that when they realized we were the police, no one ran. Folk gang members were "beating in" in a new member. The festivities had just started when we showed up, so the prospective banger didn't look too bad. Ricky asked him if he wanted to do it. He said, "More than anything. I ain't nothin' without them." We got in the car and went around the block. Ricky parked, and we watched for about three minutes as they took turns punching and kicking him. When they finished beating him in, each one of them hugged him. Ricky

Move Along; Nothing to See Here

said, "Even if we had stopped it tonight, the kid would have done it eventually anyway." I agreed with him.

One busy night, dispatch called a sergeant to advise him they were holding a loud music complaint. The caller advised there was a large party at a house. Ricky and I volunteered to take the call. When we arrived we recognized several of the vehicles that were parked along the street. Ricky looked at me as we got out of the car and said, "These are black folks, gang bangers, let me do the talking." I said, "Okay."

We encountered several people on the front porch, and Ricky asked who lived in the house. They looked toward the door and walked away. We went inside. The music was extremely loud, and there were about twenty people dancing in the living room. We stood there for a minute looking around. Someone found the guy who lived there, and Ricky motioned for him to come outside. Ricky told him we had gotten a complaint and asked him to turn the music down. He said no problem, and went inside and turned it down low enough that Ricky was pleased, so we left.

After we left, Ricky said, "Did you see that?" I wasn't sure what he was talking about so I said, "What?" He said, "I went in the house, didn't have to say a word, and homeboy turned the music down." I told him I could have done that and asked if he wanted a medal. He said, "I'm just trying to show you how it's done." I said. "Okay, your awesome—get over yourself." He laughed and asked me how many white garbage truck crew members I knew. I told him I didn't know, but I would count them next time I saw them.

One night in Roger Williams we spotted a stolen car and tried to stop it. The driver stopped and took off on foot through the projects. Ricky took off after him, and I drove around the corner to cut him off. Ricky met me at the end of the block. No bad guy. We figured he ran into an apartment or doubled back on us. We went back to the car, but it was gone. Neither one of us had notified dispatch what was going on, so we decided to keep it between us. As I was about to drive

Darrell McMann

away, the same car passed us. We sat there for moment stunned and took off after it. The car stopped again, and the driver took off running again. It appeared as if it was planned, so we decided to just impound the car.

January of 1994 became extremely dangerous for JoJo's neighbors in the Bottoms. JoJo had acquired a 45-caliber handgun and was committing at least one armed robbery a day. His cohorts, as well as everyone else in the neighborhood, were afraid of him. Ron, Ricky, and I hunted him for over a week. Ron found out JoJo was running to a vacant house close by after he had mugged someone. Ricky and I were flagged down by a neighborhood store owner one night. He told us JoJo had just threatened him with a gun and told him he would be back. We told the store owner we would park down the street. We told him to signal us when JoJo came back.

A few minutes later we noticed him signaling us. I drove slowly down the street without any lights on. When I entered the intersection and looked down the street we saw JoJo standing in the middle of the street with a gun in his hand. He saw us and took off on foot. I accelerated, and Ricky yelled for me to stop when we got to where we thought JoJo was. As Ricky was getting out, I checked my side mirror and saw JoJo crouching between two parked cars behind us. He was raising the gun. I yelled to Ricky that he was behind us. Jo Jo heard me and took off running again. Ricky took off after him on foot, and I drove around the corner to cut him off. I got to the next intersection and didn't see them. Ricky got on the radio and told me JoJo had doubled back around a house. I turned around, and I saw JoJo run back across the street. Ricky was about twenty-five feet behind him. I heard a gunshot and saw the muzzle flash from JoJo's gun. Ricky hit the dirt, and I knew he had been shot. I ran to him expecting something terrible, but he was getting up when I reached him. He said he was about twenty feet behind JoJo when he fired a round at him. He heard it whiz by his head and thought he was dead until he heard me yelling. We searched the area for about an hour but didn't find him.

Move Along; Nothing to See Here

JoJo was caught a few days later hiding underneath a carnival trailer at Mardi Gras.

Mardi Gras 1994 was somewhat boring for us. Our assignment was to patrol the perimeter of the north side of the parade route and basically look for troublemakers walking to the Mardi Gras parades. Two plain-clothes officers were shot at close range while attempting to make an arrest during a parade. Both officers nearly bled to death as the ambulance tried to make its way out of downtown. They both recovered and eventually returned to duty.

Ricky was a close friend of one of the officers. The department received word that some gang bangers might try to kill them while they were in the hospital. We smuggled some guns in even though the department sent a couple of officers to guard them.

Joe Cain day is the Sunday before Mardi Gras Day. There are several parades during the day, and throughout the day, people are getting drunker by the minute. Bienville Square usually turns into a huge wrestling ring every year. Ricky and I kept hearing the major call for more crowd-control units at the square, so we decided to go check it out. We parked and got our riot helmets and batons out of the trunk. When we got to the park we saw eight mounted officers watching a large crowd in the park. There were twenty officers standing behind them along the sidewalk. We asked the last officer in line what was going on. He said when the sergeant, who was on a horse, blew his whistle, the mounted officers would surround the fight. How the other officers would respond depended on which end of the line was closest to the fight. The first three or four officers knocked everyone down who were involved in the fight to get to the opposite end of the fight.

Within minutes the sergeant blew his whistle, and the horses took off. I was at the end of the line farthest from the fight, so I would be last one entering the ring. The plan worked just like it was supposed to. The horses surrounded the fight, and the officers on foot entered the fray. As I was entering the fight, the first guy to get knocked to

Darrell McMann

the ground was getting up. He was drunk, wasn't sure what had happened, and wasn't happy. He turned toward me, and I tackled him. I cuffed him, and we walked the prisoners out of the park with the horses shielding us.

I got to the sidewalk and noticed the major walking over to me, so I stopped. He looked at my prisoner and said, "Didn't I tell you to leave!" The prisoner said, "Yeah, Uncle Roy, but I had to stay with my friends." I thought this is just great. His nephew had dirt caked in his nose, a bloody lip, and grass clippings all over him. The major looked at me and told me to take the cuffs off. He told his nephew to leave or he would put his ass in jail himself. The major patted me on the shoulder, laughed, and walked away.

Ricky and I transferred back to patrol two months later. We both decided to leave when it seemed as if Barney was going out of his way to screw with Ricky, and we weren't satisfied with how the unit was being utilized. Barney was our supervisor most of the time considering our work schedule. I went back to my old squad, and Ricky transferred to the Fourth Precinct.

Chapter 6

When I transferred back to the squad, I wanted my old beat back, and I wanted to work next to Ron. Another officer had the beat permanently. I told Sgt. Sweat I wanted it back whenever it came open. He gave me the central beat in Toulminville, which was the next beat south of my old beat; David Garth worked the southern half of Toulminville.

David and I responded to a domestic disturbance one night when the husband threw his wife through a large plate-glass window in the front of their house. The paramedics were with her when we arrived. She had a very large laceration on her head, and she had lost a large amount of blood. We went to the front door and found the screen door was locked. The husband was sitting in his Lazy Boy watching TV; I asked him to come out and talk to me, but he refused. I asked him what happened, and he responded that he didn't know, and it was none of my business. I told him he needed to unlock the door. He told me where I could go and what I should do when I got there. I grabbed the handle of the screen door and tried to open it, but it broke off in my hand, which really got him going; he went to the back of the house.

Another guy was sitting on the couch next to the door, so I asked him to unlock the door. He told me he didn't have anything to do with it and just sat there. Since the assault was a felony, I took out my pocketknife, cut the screen; I reached in, and unlocked the door. David and I went in and found the guy in his bedroom. I told the guy he was under arrest, and to turn around and put his hands behind his back. He decided he wanted to fight. He rushed toward me and tried to spear me like a linebacker, but I sidestepped him, and he ran into the wall. I grabbed him, and David tried to cuff him, but he went crazy and started running backward into the wall and a china cabinet. When I lost my balance and let go of him, he ran back into his bedroom. He turned as I entered the room, and we exchanged a couple of punches.

Move Along; Nothing to See Here

David came over the top of me and hit him in the forehead with his aluminum baton. Blood was gushing from his head, and it looked like his head had exploded. He backed up, wiped his head, and looked at his hand. "You have done it now!" he said as he came toward us again. David struck him three or four times on his thighs, and he dropped to the ground, with me on top of him. It took us another minute or two to cuff him. The three of us stood up and noticed we were in the living room in front of the broken window. Half the neighborhood was standing in the street watching the fight. No one gave us any problems since they knew what he had done and had watched us try to arrest him. His friend was nowhere in sight.

I arrested a guy one night in Toulminville for cocaine possession. After I cuffed him he said, "Every time I see you, you lockin' up a brutha!" I said, "Really?" He said, "Yeah, man." I asked him how long he had been seeing me, and he replied, "Two or three years." I said, "So you have been seeing me for two or three years?" He said, "That's right." I said, "And I'm always arresting a black person?" He said, "That's right. You don't like black folks." I said, "So I don't like black folks?" He said, "That's right. That's what I said." I asked him, "Who lives in Toulminville?" He said, "Black folks." I said, "So if you have been seeing me for two or three years, working in Toulminville, where black people live, I would more than likely be arresting black people. If I worked out in West Mobile or down on Dauphin Island Parkway, I would be arresting white people." He told me he had never thought about it that way. I asked him if he still thought I didn't like black people. He said, "I don't know you, man." I pointed out that he didn't know me two minutes ago when he made his comment. He said, "Now you confusing me, you messy."

I started responding frequently to a house in Toulminville, where a single mother with an infant was living with her parents. The first time I met them was at two in the morning. The mother was drunk and wanted to leave. She wanted to take the baby with her, but her parents wouldn't let her take the baby. When I arrived, she was screaming and was very belligerent. She told me she was leaving. I told her she was an adult and could leave if she wanted to. She said she wanted to take her baby with her. I told her she was too drunk to take the baby with her, but she wanted to argue. I knew if I left her, I or someone else would have to come back later. I asked her to come outside, which she did. I walked out to the street, and when we reached the street, I arrested her for public intoxication. Before I left, her parents thanked me, and I advised them to get custody of the baby.

Five days later I responded to the same house for the same circumstances at about the same time of the morning. I walked in the house, and she was holding the baby. She was drunk again and wanted to leave. I told her she could leave, but the baby had to stay. She started screaming at her mother. The mother told me they had been granted temporary custody and showed me the court order. She also told me they wanted her out of the house. All the daughter's clothing and personal items were in garbage bags piled next to the front door. I told the daughter that it was time for her to go, but the baby needed to stay. She told me she was taking the baby. I told her she was about to go to jail for something a lot bigger than being drunk, and I told her she would pay dearly if the baby got hurt. She took a few steps toward the door, and I yelled at her to think about what she was doing. She stopped briefly and took another step. I grabbed her shoulders and told her mother to get the baby. She must have had a moment of clarity and allowed her mother to take the baby. I cuffed her and took her to jail. Before I left, I told her parents to put the garbage bags outside the fence next to the sidewalk. She would be able to get them when she got out of jail.

Two weeks later I got another early morning call to the same house. They heard someone trying to get in the house and locked themselves in the bedroom. I arrived and the parents were standing at the front door screaming for me to come in the house. Their daughter was drunk and crawled under the house. She knocked a hole in the floor in the bathroom and got in the house. She tried to get away back through the floor when she realized the police had arrived. Her getaway plan didn't work—she got stuck. She attempted to dive through the opening in the floor head first but forgot about the cross members. I walked in and found her feet sticking straight up as she

Move Along; Nothing to See Here

was trying to make her getaway. I had to pull her free and arrested her again. Her parents moved a few weeks later, and I never heard from them again.

We had a representative from one of the city's civic organizations give a presentation at one of our roll calls. The organization was attempting to make life better for some of Mobile's citizens. She told us we needed to encourage the children in our beats to do the best they possibly could and not get discouraged when things didn't go their way. She passed out buttons that read Be The Best You That You Can Be. We were all quiet for about a minute as we looked at these buttons. The lieutenant finally asked, "Anyone have any questions?" Ron said, "I don't have any questions, but I have a few observations. Are we supposed to give out these buttons after we arrest daddy for beating momma? During domestics while mom and dad are screaming and cussing each at other? Across the street from a homicide while everyone in the neighborhood is going crazy? Or do you want us to hand these buttons out as they are walking down the street thinking about when or if they are going to get to eat dinner tonight? The representative wasn't anticipating questions like that and didn't know what to say. One of the sergeants said, "We will get back with you on that." We went to work. We never received any further instructions on the button distribution.

I was dispatched to one of the gay bars downtown in reference to a couple of street preachers yelling at couples entering the bar. I contacted the owner who was extremely upset. He told me he didn't have a problem with freedom of speech or freedom of religion, but he had issues with the mean-spiritedness of their comments, which were upsetting some of his customers. I told him I would speak with them.

As I walked across the street I wasn't looking forward to the conversation I was about to have. I contacted the street preachers and told them why I was there. They of course started getting defensive about their freedom of speech and freedom of religion. I assured them I had no intention of denying them their constitutional rights.

Darrell McMann

I said, "You need to keep something in mind." The preacher in charge asked, "What is that?" I said, "Ya'll have to remember that even though they are gay, they are still men. Some of them are big men. Some of them will hurt you. You need to remember that." He said, "Officer, you have a point. We will tone it down and not be as hateful." I left.

Later the owner of the bar called dispatch and asked for me to call him. I called him, and he said, "I don't know what you told them, but they are one hundred percent more respectful. Thank you."

From time to time citizens will request to ride along with an officer. I had several that were cop groupies. I couldn't wait until the end of the shift to get rid of them. I didn't mind someone riding with me if he or she wanted to see how the police department operated and how things really worked. I had a black female who came out with me on a Friday night on the evening shift. She had no idea how the north side of Mobile really was. She lived in a nice neighborhood in West Mobile. We drove through the bottoms. She couldn't believe all the people that were walking around. I commented that a lot of people in this neighborhood didn't own cars. We responded to Roger Williams for a loud music complaint. I turned the corner onto Brazier. There were at least 150 people in the street and twenty cars playing music. She said, "OH, MY GOD!" when I parked. As I was getting out of the cruiser, she said, "WHERE ARE YOU GOING?" I said, "I need to talk to everyone about the music." She locked the doors. I came back a few minutes later. "Why is everyone still out?" she asked. "I didn't ask them to leave. I just had them turn the music down," I replied. "So you're going to leave them here?" she asked. "Most of them live here. Where do you suggest they go?" She didn't say anything.

We heard several shots fired in the Bottoms and drove the area looking. She couldn't slide any lower in her seat.

Our last call was for a female that was screaming. I found her in the middle of the street. Her boyfriend had been avoiding the drug dealer he owed money to for several weeks. The drug dealer and two of his buddies found him at her house in Prichard. They dragged them

Move Along; Nothing to See Here

out of the house to the drainage ditch. The drug dealer and one of his buddies beat the boyfriend while the other guy held his girlfriend. They got tired of beating him up and decided to gang rape the girlfriend while holding him at gunpoint. When they were finished, the drug dealer said, "Don't worry about my money, you're paid up." They left. The girlfriend ran into Toulminville screaming. They were both bloody and scared to death. I called for a Prichard officer to join me. They both told me they didn't want to report it. The Prichard officer showed up, and they told him they didn't need him and walked away.

My ride along couldn't believe the story and was shocked they didn't want anything done. I told her, "It happens everyday." She thanked me for the eye-opening experience.

It was the end of July, when I got a domestic disturbance call in Toulminville. My backup and I parked in front of the neighbor's house. When I got out I could see a black female standing in the backyard. She saw me and made a quick movement with her right hand. I heard what sounded like a small caliber gunshot, so as she ran down the driveway, I pulled my gun out and yelled at her to stop. The hedgerow along the driveway prevented me from having a good view of her, but when I moved toward the end of the hedgerow, I could see she didn't have anything in her hands. She was wearing blue jean shorts, a white T-shirt, and no shoes. When I reached out to grab her as she was running by me, I heard the back door of the house slam. A black male ran around the corner of the house toward us, screaming, "YOU BLACK BITCH! I'M GOING TO F'N KILL YOU!" I directed my attention toward him and yelled for my backup to get the woman. I was in a better position to see that the male wasn't armed, he was in his underwear, and I attempted to grab him as I was holstering my gun, but he got by me.

The female was standing in the street between our cruisers. The male saw her and went straight for her; he jumped toward her to tackle her, but before he hit her, she removed an eight-inch serrated knife from her waistband and threw it at him. He knocked her to the ground, got on top of her, and punched her three times before I could

Darrell McMann

get him off of her. I had a good arm-bar hold on him and was backing away from the street. He said, "Okay, I'm done. The bitch had it coming. I'll do whatever you want." Meanwhile, the female, who was about twenty feet from us, got up and with all her power ran into us. I was falling backward and let him go because I didn't want him on top of me.

She jumped in the front seat of my cruiser, and he followed her. They continued their fight in the front seat of my cruiser. She found my baton and hit him in the head a couple of times. My backup was basically tapping the male on the shoulder and pleading with him to stop. I brushed past her and grabbed him around his neck. We wore Velcro inner and outer belts at the time, and something in the door jam caught the end of my belt. I could hear the Velcro coming loose and felt my belt hit the ground. I looked and saw my gun on the ground; I yelled for my backup to get my gun and call for help. She called for help but didn't get my gun.

I backed away from the door, and he started telling me was done. I saw the female was to my left and noticed she had bent down. She walked in front of me and raised my gun toward the male. I yelled for my backup to shoot her and tried to get my 38 out of my ankle holster while trying to use the male as a shield. He didn't like the position he was in and was struggling really hard. I realized that my backup had pulled her weapon because it seemed like she was trying to rest it on my shoulder. The female lost her nerve and walked back to the house. I bulldogged the male to the ground, and managed to get a good chicken-wing hold on him. I decided I would rest for a second before trying to handcuff him. I was wondering why someone else wasn't trying to cuff him. I could hear sirens in the distance, so I decided to wait until someone else showed up before doing anything else. The first person to show up was the SWAT team commander, Lt. Kelly. He helped me cuff the guy.

I put him in my backseat and asked my backup where my gun was. She said, "I guess it's in the house." I said, "GO GET IT!" She came back out and handed me my gun and stood there. I said, "Where is the

Move Along; Nothing to See Here

female?" She said, "Oh, you want her too?" I said, "YOU"VE GOT TO BE KIDDING ME." She went back and got her but didn't cuff her. I told her to cuff her and transport her for me. I could tell from Lt. Kelly's expression that he had many questions, but I guess he decided he would find out later.

The female was from Mississippi and was visiting family. She was six months pregnant and didn't know who the daddy was. The male was her brother. He told her she was a whore when he found out and that made her mad. She decided she would get him in trouble and called 911 claiming he was about to beat her. When I pulled up she threw a large rock and broke the windshield of his car.

The next day dispatch called and advised me Lt. Webb wanted me to meet him in his office. He was a little aggravated when I walked in the room and wanted to know what had happened the day before. He had just left headquarters, where he'd been asked by a major and a captain why one of his officers allowed another officer to be undressed by a suspect and a second suspect ended up with an officer's gun. I explained the whole incident to him. He wanted to know what my backup was doing. I said, "I didn't know she was behind me I couldn't see what she was doing." He asked if I was okay. I said I was but my wife was mad because I lost my wedding band during the fight. He said, "We'll see if the city will replace it." He told me something might come of this, so don't tell to many people what's going on.

I found my backup from the previous day and told her questions were being asked at headquarters. I told her what Lt. Webb said. I also told her I couldn't answer the question of what she was doing because I didn't know. She told me thanks and drove away. At the end of the month, she was moved to a "tamer" beat in the precinct, and I got my old beat back. I ordered belt keepers the day after the incident.

Chapter 7

Sgt Sweat asked me if I wanted to be an FTO again a few weeks after I got my favorite beat back; I told him I would do it. A couple of weeks later I met my next trainee, Mark Finer. Mark was a quick learner, he enjoyed being proactive, and he could handle criticism.

One night Mark and I were leaving a call in the Bottoms near Patton Avenue; I remembered George. I told Mark we were going to try and get a gun. We parked about a block and a half away and walked quietly down the street. We made it to a large tree two houses away and saw George out by the road saying good-bye to some family members. I told Mark we would wait till they left. The car left, and George watched it go down the street. I waited until he looked away before running toward him. We got within fifty feet of him before he realized we were there. We had our guns drawn and were yelling at him to get on the ground. He ran toward the side of the house, but we were on top of him. As I tackled him he attempted to take a gun out of his waistband and throw it under the house. The gun hit the side of the house and landed about six inches from his hand. Luckily he didn't see it and try to do something stupid. After a brief struggle we were able to cuff him. Ron pulled up to us as we walked him back to the cruiser. We fist bumped, and he told me he knew eventually one of us would get him. George looked at him and told him it wasn't his old ass. Ron told him it didn't matter who got him, he was going to prison.

The address 251 Rollins Street became very familiar to me. An older couple in their late fifties that argued constantly and stayed drunk lived there. They or their neighbors called frequently. I found the husband passed out in the yard several times and helped him into the house and plopped him down on the couch. One of them called one night because they were arguing and very drunk. She wanted him to leave, and he wanted her to leave. Neither one of them wanted to leave, so they decided they would get along. Thirty minutes later,

Move Along; Nothing to See Here

I got a second call about this couple; it was an extremely busy night and I was in no mood for their trash. I got out of the cruiser and approached them on the porch. Before they could say anything, I told them I had had enough of them for tonight. If I had to come back, I would put one or both of them in jail. They said they were sorry and went inside. I got a third call about thirty minutes later. The female told the dispatcher that her husband was lying on the porch and she thought he had been shot. I acknowledged the call and dispatch sent me a backup. I canceled the backup, telling dispatch that they were drunk when I left them thirty minutes ago, and he probably passed out.

I pulled up in front of the house and saw the husband lying on his back on the porch; his head was next to the front door. I walked up and noticed he had a large goose egg on his forehead. His wife said, "I think he's been shot." I said, "He ain't been shot. I knew one day he would fall and hurt himself." His wife was standing in the house, and the screen door was closed. The paramedics showed up and as I was talking to her through the screen door, they started checking his vitals. His wife said, "I think he's been shot." Before I could answer her, the paramedic said, "Hey officer, this guy has been shot." I turned around, and the paramedic lifted his eyelid and discovered there was no eye. He said, "He's dead," and they started CPR. I looked at the screen and noticed a hole where he would have been standing. I gave the screen a quick inspection with my flashlight and found no other holes. I went inside, and before I could say anything, she said, "I think he's been shot." I looked down just inside the door and found the gun on the floor behind the TV. I called dispatch and advised that I had a homicide. Major crimes and crime scene responded. Sgt. Sweat came to the scene. He said, "I thought you said he was drunk." I whispered that technically he was drunk, but now he was dead.

At the end of 1994, Lt. Webb retired and was replaced by Lt. Lonnie Cox. Lt. Webb was great to work for, but I didn't know Lonnie and had never met him. I heard he was good to work for, so I was a little relieved. I had a couple of veteran officers on a different shift tell me he was biased against white officers, and I should be careful. I didn't give

Darrell McMann

it much thought because of who it came from and decided not worry about it. It didn't take long to see he was going to be great to work for.

Sgt. Sweat was promoted to lieutenant and was transferred to another precinct. Rob Yonkley and Carl Wilson transferred to our squad. They were both great to work for and I felt blessed that I didn't work for spastic bosses. Tony and Mark stayed on our squad when they completed the FTO program. We were joined by a few rookies—Ted Severs and John Tipple. They would eventually work the Toulminville beats; we worked a lot of calls together and became good friends. My academy classmate, Steve Banks, had been on the squad from the beginning, and he worked the Happy Hills beat. Ron was still working the eastern end of MLK and Orange Grove. Steve, Ron, and I worked together closely. Greg Mass, who was kind of quiet but a great officer, worked the area south of Roy. Bart Mathews joined us in the summer, and it was good to work with him again. We became friends after I completed the FTO program. Wade Brantley and several other officers on our squad that I worked with from time to time were also very good officers. It was nice to work with people who didn't embarrass you on calls by the way they acted. We had a great squad, and we all enjoyed working together.

Nineteen ninety-four was a bad year for patrol cars. Chief Nagin decided to have the stereos removed from the new patrol cars that had just arrived. In his words, "They ain't smart enough to listen to a stereo, portable radio, in-car radio, operate the computer, and drive a car at the same time." It cost additional money to remove the stereos. I wondered who the moron was.

We also had several police officers involved traffic crashes because of speeding and carelessness. The chief ordered dispatch to remind us to "watch your speed" after we acknowledged calls. We thought that was stupid. I would say, "Ten four, and I'm watching my speed." I felt like I was being dispatched by my parents.

The chief went to the city garage and tried to order them to notify him when the cars were repaired. He didn't want them to release the

Move Along; Nothing to See Here

cars back to the precincts until he decided to release them. The director at the garage told him he must have forgotten that the garage owns the cars, and he needed to go back to his office. I didn't understand the chief's line of thinking. If we had several cars that were down, it hurt our response time because we were working two-man cars.

I was creeping though the neighborhood on the south side of MLK near Orange Grove late one night, when I turned the corner and saw a male make a sweeping motion with his arm toward a female; they were standing in the middle of the street. He took off running when he heard me coming. I wasn't sure what happened until I drove up behind her. She turned and ran to me before I could get out of the car. She stuck her head through my window and yelled that she thought she'd been cut. I leaned as far as I could to the right. He had cut her with a butcher knife across the right side of her forehead. She was bleeding profusely, and the skin was peeled back exposing her skull. She was cracked out and couldn't feel anything. I thought I was an extra in a horror film and used the door to back her up, so I could get out. Steve found the guy hiding under a house within a few minutes. We never found the butcher knife.

For some reason, it seemed like every driver I stopped said, "You are stopping me because I'm black." I finally got tired of it. I pulled over a car and approached the driver. I said, "Do you know why I'm stopping you?' He said, "Yeah, because I'm black." I said, "Yeah, your right. You have stumbled upon a major conspiracy." The Mobile Police Department stops only black people. Don't tell anyone because we want to keep it a secret." He stared at me for a few seconds and didn't know what to say. He gave me his license, and I wrote him a ticket. When he signed the ticket, he looked at me said, "You ain't right." "What do you mean?" I asked. "I know I deserve a ticket. I was trying to make you feel guilty but you got the best of me," he replied.

The next night, I made a traffic stop on a vehicle on Patton Avenue. The driver exited the vehicle—actually he unfolded out of the car. He was the biggest man I had ever seen, and he was nothing but muscle. I asked him if he knew why I stopped him. He had a very deep voice, so it sounded like he roared when he said, "You stopped me because I'm black!" I replied, "Come on, look at me and look at you. Why on earth would I stop you for that? You could squash me like a bug. I would have to call out the SWAT team if you gave me any trouble. I stopped you because your taillights are out." He looked at me for a minute, told me he was sorry, and explained that he had a bad day. I told him we all had those days. He had a good license, so I let him go home with a warning. He thanked me, apologized again, and went home.

One Saturday night I was stopped at the red light at Anne and Congress. I noticed a pickup truck on Anne heading toward MLK. What made me take notice were the two white guys in the back of the truck holding up a large Confederate flag. They were also trying to give a spirited rendition of their best rebel yell. I decided I should probably watch to see where they were going. They turned onto MLK and headed west toward Roger Williams. I thought I better stop them before they got themselves killed. The truck made a quick turn and circled the block. They got back on MLK. I turned on my lights and pulled them over.

I walked up to the truck and contacted the driver. The guys in the back of the truck stood looking forward holding the flag. The driver asked, "Officer, what is the problem?" I said, "I'm trying to prevent a homicide." He said, "Whose homicide?" I said, "Yours or one of your friends." He said, "Why would we be in danger?" I said, "Don't be stupid. You are driving around MLK with a giant Confederate flag, and your buddies are doing their best rebel yells." I happened to notice I had stopped them in front of the Amvets club. The driver said, "Don't we have free speech?" I said, "Sure you do." Most of the people in the club had come out to the sidewalk. I said, "Look to your left. What do you think they think about your freedom of speech? Ya'll can do whatever you want. I have a feeling ya'll are about to create some work for me. I think I'll just leave, and ya'll can practice your freedom of speech with them." A couple of the patrons on the sidewalk said, "Yeah, Baby Adams just leave we will take care of those white boys."

Move Along; Nothing to See Here

The two guys in the back of the truck sat down. The driver said, "I think I see what you're talking about. I think we will leave." I said, "So, you have seen the error of your ways?" He said, "Yes sir."

I responded to a domestic argument one afternoon on MLK. The husband was drunk and mad about something his wife supposedly did. Her brother was there and was trying to talk to him, but he didn't want to listen to anything he had to say. The husband had no interest in anything I had to say either. The wife talked him into going in the house to chill out. He was headed inside when a neighbor from across the street asked me to come speak to them. He decided to sit on the porch to watch our conversation.

The neighbors told me the husband was making threats to the female before I got there. He told her he was going to hurt her after the police left and would kill her brother if he tried anything. They said her brother showed up to return something he borrowed and walked into the middle of it. They said he tried to talk to him, but he shoved him just before I showed up. The brother walked over and told me he would try and take his sister with him to keep anything from happening. I said okay. The female was next door, so I walked over to talk to her. She agreed to leave with her brother. While speaking with her, her brother and husband met in the middle of the street.

I walked over to them and was about to tell the husband what was going to happen when he threw a punch at his brother-in-law that narrowly missed me. They fell to ground at my feet fighting. The brother-in-law ended up on top and was wearing him out. I put my hand on his shoulder and told him to stop. The husband's hands were trapped under his knees, so he stopped hitting him. I told him to get off of him. He said okay. When he moved his knees, the husband's hands came free, and he punched him a couple times before he was able to get control of him again. He hit him several times and stopped when I told him to. He told me he wasn't going to let him go again, so he could get punched. I didn't blame him.

Darrell McMann

I looked around and saw a couple of young guys standing in the yard watching us. I asked them to come over. I told one of them to grab the guy on top and take him to the other side of the yard. I told them not to hurt him but just take him over there. He said okay.

The second guy looked at me and smiled. He said, "I know what I get to do. You and me are going beat him down." I said, "No we aren't going to do that. I'm going to grab an arm just before he gets off of him and turn him over then cuff him." He said, "Yeah, man, but what am I going to do?" I said, "You are my backup." He said, "Oh, I see, if you need help, I can beat him down then." I said, "That's right." He smiled. My backup happened to be about six-feet-five and 260 pounds with muscles stacked on top of muscles. The husband heard our conversation, saw his future opponent, and offered no resistance.

Ron and I were on evenings when we responded to three shootings in Roger Williams on consecutive nights. We knew it was a rival gang, but we didn't know which one. The suspect(s) would park on St. Charles and walk through the wooded lot. See a group of Roger Williams gangsters and fire a few rounds at them and run back to their car. No one had been hit yet and no one had seen anyone creeping around.

Roy had backed me on a call in Roger Williams when we saw Strawberry and a couple of his Blood soldiers; we parked and walked up to them. One of the guys said he was tired of the police messing with them about the shootings. I asked him who was messing with them. He said, "Those Ranger assholes." Strawberry told him to chill out and that they ain't Rangers. He looked at me and said, "I've seen you around for a while. You lock a brutha up if you have to, but you fair, and you ain't lookin' to do us dirty." He said, "I've seen you get pissed at the Rangers because they messin' with us when there ain't no reason to." I just nodded. What I didn't tell him is that I was trying to build a good rapport, but the Rangers would swoop in and mess it up for me for a couple of weeks. They were just doing what they were supposed to do. He looked at Ron and smiled. He said, "Everyone knows you, Adams."

Move Along; Nothing to See Here

"You see how nobody is out here, everyone is inside?" Strawberry asked. "They scared." Ron asked him if he had heard anything. Strawberry thought for a minute. He said, "I think it's a Toulminville gang banger." He gave us a description of a vehicle and told us where he thought the guy lived. Ron asked him why they hadn't retaliated. He said, "I just found out about five minutes before ya'll walked up." One of his guys was pissed and asked, "You gonna trust these bitches to do something for us?" He said, "Yeah, WE are." I asked him to give us an hour, and I would get back to him.

We found the guy's house, but he was off with some friends. We got his name and found out he had several outstanding arrest warrants; we notified investigations. I went back to Roger Williams and told Strawberry what we found out, leaving out the guys name and address. He asked, but I smiled and told him I couldn't do that. He thanked me and told me he owed me. The shooter was arrested the next day.

I responded to an apartment in Roger Williams one night and noticed a puddle of some type of juice on the floor; it looked like it had been there for at least a day. The juice had coagulated. There were a couple of flies and a roach struggling to free themselves from it; I almost felt sorry for them. The lady noticed I was looking at the puddle and said, "I haven't had time to clean just been so busy." I looked around and noticed all the empty beer cans and food wrappers on the floor. I said, "Oh yeah, I know what you mean."

I walked out to my cruiser to get paperwork for a report. As I started walking back to the apartment I heard the unmistakable sound of the hammer slamming home on a revolver. I crouched and spun around while pulling my gun. I took cover behind my cruiser. I heard it again and heard two people laughing. I called for some backup. When my backup arrived, we found two guys high from smoking weed laced with PCP playing Russian roulette in the doorway of an apartment across the street with a 357 Magnum. One of them had forgotten to load it. It didn't matter because it was stolen.

There was a guy who walked MLK everyday carrying a Bible and yelling Bible verses; I had never spoken with him, until one day when he walked up to my cruiser as I was sitting in a parking lot on MLK writing a report. I put my paperwork down and got out of the car. He stood about twenty feet away and didn't say anything; we stared at each other for about thirty seconds. I finally asked him if I could help him. He said, "I don't follow man's law. I follow God's law! I don't have to follow any orders or instructions you give me!" I said, "Is that so?" He nodded yes. I said, "When I became a police officer I took an oath before God. God commands people to obey those placed in authority above us. Did you know that?" He turned and walked away.

Working in an inner city neighborhood with a crack problem gave me the opportunity to be around prostitutes, and I soon realized that most of them were addicted to crack. We had white hookers, black hookers, transvestites in various stages of shedding their boy parts, and cross dressers. Most of the transvestites peddled their wares in the First Precinct, which was downtown. It's a rough life to live. We would find them beaten on the side of the street—a few of them had been shot or stabbed. It was impossible for patrol to keep them off the street corners because of the heavy volume of calls, the gang members we tried to monitor, and the dope spots we were working. They usually were respectful to us and knew we would stop to help them if we saw someone giving them a hard time. Every once in a while I would watch one from a distance and follow the car that picked her up; I would look for a reason to stop the vehicle. I usually ended up with a dope and or a gun arrest; most of the Johns had warrants or bad driver licenses. We couldn't stop a vehicle for picking someone up even though we knew the female was prostitute. If they were waving cars down, we would stop and talk to them and make them go home. They didn't have to wave anyone down because there were always plenty of customers cruising the area.

I stopped a car one night on Patton Avenue that had a prostitute in it. The driver tried to tell me they were old friends and came up with a name and said they were going to a friend's house. I let him talk for

Move Along; Nothing to See Here

several minutes and broke the news to him. I told him I knew her, told him what her name was, and that I knew she was a prostitute; he got quiet. I told him I had watched him drive by her three times, and that he had stopped when she stepped into the street. I asked him where his friend lived; he admitted he was lying. I told her to get out and go home. She told him thanks for the $20 and left. I searched him, and the vehicle but didn't find anything. He had no warrants, and his license was good. I wondered aloud how he was going to tell his wife he had contracted HIV from a prostitute, and I walked away. When I left, he was standing outside his car crying. I never saw him again.

Surprisingly we had very few problems with the prostitutes fighting with each other. They seemed to work in pairs and had their sections they worked. One of them flagged me down one night and told me a new black girl was working. She said she was going to get hurt if someone didn't tell her how things worked; I found her a few minutes later. I wouldn't have guessed she was working because she was well dressed and clean; she told me she was trying to earn money for college. She wanted to become an artist. She had a backpack with her and showed me some of her drawings, which were very good. She hadn't been out for very long and hadn't been picked up yet. I asked her if she had applied for a grant. She didn't know what that was, so I explained it to her. I told her to go to Bishop State down the street Monday morning and talk to someone; she told me she would. She thanked me and told me she was happy I stopped her because she was really scared; she hugged me and went home. I'm assuming she got a grant and went to college because I never saw her again.

We would get flagged down by prostitutes for what we called *felony failure to pay*. It usually happened to rookie prostitutes. They would provide their services before getting paid. The John would shove them out of the car when she finished without paying for services rendered. The John and the prostitute would have a disagreement over payment for services rendered. The prostitute would grab the wallet or the cash in his hand and take off and the John would try to report it as a robbery. It was funny to watch them try and come up

Darrell McMann

with a story that would explain how the female was able to get the money. They would have a hard time coming up with a plausible reason why their zipper was down and what they were doing in the area.

There were two clubs on my beat that used constables for security. The constable is a peace officer, elected by the voting precinct but has jurisdiction throughout the county. The constable has full arrest powers, essentially the same as the sheriff. The constable has the authority to enforce both the traffic code and the criminal code. They have the authority to suppress fires and to act as a forest warden. Qualifications necessary to become a constable are the same as those needed to become a sheriff. The constable is an elected public official and is one of the only two remaining elected peace officers in the world. They are not required to have any formal training.

There was a fight at one of the clubs on MLK that used a couple of constables. We were told a couple of them were claiming to be Mobile police officers. We told them they couldn't wear shirts with the word *police* on the back, so they switched to *sheriff* but with two Rs. We thought it was funny and failed to point out they had misspelled sheriff. We also heard they would beat people for not leaving the club fast enough when they were thrown out. No one ever complained about it, and we never saw anything.

The club let out one night, and a fight started out front. There were two constables working the club, and they weren't having much success getting the crowd to move on. One of them took out his .45 and started shooting in the air. He leveled his aim and fired a few shots down MLK. One of them hit a young female three blocks away. She was dead by the time I got there; the constable went to prison for manslaughter. The club quit using constables and closed down.

Another club on St. Stephens Road, located in a strip mall near Three Mile Creek also used constables. I was flagged down one night by a couple in a jeep. The guy told me he was asked to leave by a constable, so he walked outside. Someone went to get his girlfriend in the bathroom, and when she came out they left. As they were

Move Along; Nothing to See Here

leaving the parking lot, the constable fired several shots at them but didn't hit anything. They didn't want a report but wanted someone to know.

The next night someone was driving by the club and called 911 when they heard a gunshot. Ron and I pulled into the parking lot and saw a large crowd at the front door. A guy walked over to us, told us the constables were crazy, and walked away. The front door flew open and two constables were escorting a guy out. They told the guy he was under arrest. The guy told them he wasn't going to jail and turned around. One of the constables attempted to pepper spray him but he missed. The three of them fell to the ground fighting. Ron whispered to me to not get involved unless it was absolutely necessary, and I was content to just watch. They eventually cuffed the guy, when they stood up, they were all bleeding.

One of the constables opened the back door of a Lincoln and put his prisoner in the backseat. He looked at Ron and told him he needed us to transport his prisoner to the hospital. Ron said, "Nope, you caught him, and you can clean him." The constable got pretty mad but didn't say anything. He thought about it for a few minutes, got his prisoner out of the car, took the cuffs off, and told him to leave. His prisoner started threatening to kill him; I walked over to him and told him he was missing out on some money. He quit him screaming and looked at me. I told him he could sue the constable for false arrest, assault, false imprisonment, and a few other things. I told him to go to the hospital and get pictures taken of his injuries for documentation. Remember everyone who was here, so they can be witnesses. Monday morning find an attorney.

The guy left for the hospital happy and focused on getting paid. The constable heard what I said but didn't say anything. Ron laughed, and we left. I wrote a long statement about the problems we were having with the security at the clubs and sent it up the chain of command. I was happy and surprised to find the issue was addressed, and we didn't have any more problems.

Darrell McMann

Shots fired calls are frequent complaints in inner city neighbor-hoods. During the evening and midnight shifts, I would hear shots fired throughout the shift. Usually it was a two- or three-round burst. I referred to those as someone stepping outside and letting everyone know, "Hey, I have a gun!" I learned not to worry about it unless you heard a whizzing bullet.

Weed and Seed had an office in a trailer on MLK. It was about 5:30 A.M., and I had purchased a newspaper, backed up to the privacy fence, and killed the cruiser's engine. I was there for about ten min-utes, when the guy who lived behind the office stepped out into his backyard and fired off three rounds. He was on the other side of the fence and didn't see me. When I forced my heart out of my throat I bailed out of the cruiser and went around the corner. The gate was open, and the guy was reloading the gun. He was shocked to see me and dropped the gun. On the way to jail, he told me he found some bullets and wanted to see if they worked.

Carjackings and strong-armed robberies were an everyday occur-rence. A disabled elderly man was getting out of his car in his drive-way in Toulminville when a gang banger stuck a gun to his head and ordered him out of the car. The old man told him he needed his walker out of the backseat and that he could have anything he wanted. The dirt bag opened the back door and got the walker. When he turned around he discovered the old man kept a 38 under his seat. He was dead before he hit the ground. DRT—dead right there.

One night, at the end of the shift, I responded to Happy Hills for a stolen vehicle complaint. The complainant met me at my cruiser. She told me her boyfriend had taken her car without her permission, and she'd thought it had been stolen. "So it's okay that he took it?" I asked. She said, "Yeah. I just didn't know he took it when I called."

While we were talking I heard a female yelling, "You can't have shit in the projects!" She yelled it several times, and it seemed as if she was trying to get a reaction out of me. I asked the complainant what

Move Along; Nothing to See Here

mouth's problem was. She said she didn't know, but the lady was her neighbor and was usually drunk. I looked over and saw two guys trying to get her to go in her apartment as I started to get in my cruiser.

Mouth yelled at me, "Hey, you can't have shit in the projects!" I decided I would find out what mouth was talking about, so I walked over and asked her what was bothering her. She said, "You can't have shit in the projects." I said, "Yeah, I got that much. What are you talking about?" She said, "I gots a nineteen ninety-three and a nineteen ninety-four." I asked, "A nineteen ninety-three and a nineteen ninety-four what?" She said, "I gots a nineteen ninety-three and a nineteen ninety-four car." I said, "That's wonderful, so what is the problem?" She said, "There ain't no problem you just can't have shit in the projects. I works hard fo my money." I asked, "What do you do?" She said, "I gets a check." I said, "You work hard for your money?" She said, "Dats right." I had enough of her trash, so I said, "It must be tough sitting around twenty-three hours a day on the couch I bought you, watching the TV I bought you, in the apartment I'm paying for. Yeah my heart bleeds for you." I looked around and said loudly, "Everyone would you please give mouth a standing ovation because she works hard from the seat of her pants drinking beer and watching TV!" Everyone laughed but mouth wasn't amused. She was screaming at me at the top of her lungs as I drove away.

Shortly after we moved to Grand Bay, Kim became the assistant director of the X-Ray Department at Singing River Hospital in Pascagoula. She was extremely excited, and I was happy for her. My parents were proud of her. Her parents wanted to know how much money she was going to make.

Kim's mother caused her lots of stress. Whenever she was coming for a visit I would be grilled about what I should not tell her. I tried not to talk to her very much anyway, so it wasn't difficult to avoid bringing up certain topics with her. She didn't have any problems voicing her opinions. I usually tuned her out. She didn't like the fact that I dipped Skoal or occasionally drank a beer or two. Before her mother came over, Kim always checked the fridge to make sure it was free of beer

Darrell McMann

and made sure there weren't any wayward cans of Skoal lying around. I thought it was ridiculous but didn't say anything for a while. I finally told Kim that this was our house, and if her mother didn't like what was in it, she didn't have to visit. She didn't come too often anyway because we usually went to see her.

Our daughter, Elizabeth, was born on December 12, 1994. The doctor came into the delivery room and turned on the TV because Monday Night Football was on. The Miami Dolphins were playing the Kansas City Chiefs, and the doctor would watch the game in between telling Kim to push. I was getting a little aggravated with him, but I figured he knew what he was doing. I started watching the game, too, but I didn't miss witnessing Elizabeth's birth, which was the proudest moment of my life.

Chapter 8

As a police officer, you quickly learn to trust is your sense of smell. I responded to several houses you could smell from the street. It's difficult for me to describe. Basically it's a mixture of urine, rotting trash, and feces mixed together. When you walk in a house and gag, it's time to leave. If I could smell it from the street, I didn't go in; I would have the individuals inside come out. You get foul-odor calls, and you cringe because you know you are going to find someone who has been dead for a while.

I went to one lady's apartment for a welfare check because her friend hadn't seen or heard from her in a couple of weeks. I knocked on the door expecting the worst; she didn't answer the door. I knocked again, and she asked who it was. I told her it was the police, and that her friend was worried about her. She told me the door was unlocked and that I could come in.

When I opened the door I got an incredible whiff of rotting trash and feces. She was lying on the couch covered with a blanket. There were several empty whiskey bottles on the floor next to the couch. Pizza boxes and other food wrappers were on the coffee table and the floor next to the couch. Feces were encrusted on the floor, the couch, and the blanket; she was very drunk. I walked into the kitchen and found a pile of dishes that hadn't been washed in at least two weeks. Empty whiskey bottles and food containers were on the kitchen counter and lying on the floor. Trash was all over the floor; water bugs were in the sink, and roaches were everywhere. I walked into the bathroom and nearly threw up. Feces were everywhere and by the look of things, she was suffering from diarrhea. She had evidently run out of toilet paper and had started using towels. I called an ambulance to transport her to the hospital. When she got off the couch, the blanket was so encrusted with feces that it looked stiff as if it had been starched. She had terrible sores on her legs, buttocks, and lower back, and she was so out of it, she didn't know what was happening.

Move Along; Nothing to See Here

Just after midnight one night, Wade Brantley was driving through a neighborhood in Toulminville when he noticed the rear doors of a commercial van were open. He knew the guy who owned the business and stopped to check the van. He found a guy in the back of the van and asked him to step out. The guy stepped out, shoved Wade to the ground, and took off on foot. Wayne alerted everyone over the radio. Ted Severs saw the guy run between a couple of houses and caught up to him. Wade, two other officers, and I heard them fighting but didn't know where they were until we saw Ted's flashlight. The guy ran away again, and we saw Ted chasing him across the street. Ted tackled him again between two houses, and they got into a brief fight. Two officers jumped on top of him, and the guy immediately went prone on the ground. They got off of him, and an officer slapped him in the back of the head and said, "You don't run from the police." Another kicked him in the side. I felt like it was about to get out of control, so I said, "HEY! Someone cuff him." Everyone looked at me and realized what was happening; we cuffed him and took him to jail. I told them later that you never know who's got a video camera, and I really didn't want to sit in a federal courtroom because we roughed up some dirt bag. Everyone shook his head.

A couple of months later we were on midnights again. We were short on cars so another officer and I had to ride together in the paddy wagon. I hated to ride in the wagon because it didn't have a stereo and the cage in the back rattled like it was about to come apart. We were covering Trinity Gardens and Crichton. Greers Grocery store on Springhill Avenue in Crichton had been broken into several times over a three-week period. All the burglaries occurred between 3:00 A.M. and 5:00 A.M. There was a day care with a long driveway on the south side of Springhill directly across the street from Greers that was dark enough for us to back up in and watch the store.

We sat there for a few minutes, and my partner fell asleep. I didn't think I was tired until I woke up about a half hour later. I rubbed my eyes and thought I saw someone standing on the sidewalk in front of the store; I woke up my partner. I said, "Am I dreaming or is someone over there?" When his eyes focused, he told me I wasn't dreaming.

Darrell McMann

The guy was looking for vehicles on Springhill but couldn't see us. He picked up a large rock and threw it several times into the store's Plexiglass, but it bounced off. We were waiting until he got in before driving over. It would be easier to catch him if we trapped him in the store. He would have heard us start the engine and definitely would have heard us bouncing over curbs in the paddy wagon. He pushed on the Plexiglass several times to test how far it would give. He backed up and threw his shoulder into it almost knocking it into the store. He checked Springhill again and threw his shoulder into it again. The Plexiglass collapsed, and he climbed into the store.

We started the engine and threw it into drive. He heard us coming as we bounced over curbs into the parking lot, and he ran out of the store and toward a side street. He ducked between a couple of houses, but we were able to get a couple of other officers in the area to help set up a perimeter. We walked through a couple of yards and found him hiding under a vehicle. We were complimented for a job well done. We left out the part about us sleeping.

In September of 1995, Kim heard the director of radiology position at the hospital in Atmore, Alabama, was open; she called and scheduled an interview. She asked if I would go with her, and I agreed. We discussed moving to Atmore if she was hired. I called the Atmore Police Department and spoke with the Assistant Chief Don Mack. I told him I would be accompanying Kim on her interview and asked about the department; we talked about my qualifications. He told me to come see him after I dropped her off.

The day of her interview she was very excited and hoped I would get good news also. I dropped her off and met Chief Mack at the police department. We talked for over an hour. He told me he would like to hire me, but he wasn't expecting to have any vacancies for at least four months. He told me he thought the Brewton Police Department was hiring. He called Chief Gene Sims and told him about Kim and I. Chief Sims asked if I could come over to Brewton and see him when Kim's interview was over; I told him I would see him around 2:00 P.M.

Move Along; Nothing to See Here

I picked up Kim and told her what was going on. Brewton is only thirty miles east of Atmore.

The meeting with Chief Sims went very well, and he had two openings. He told me to call him and let him know if Kim got the position. I told her she should hear something by the end of the week, and I would let him know either way. Kim was offered the position three days later; I knew they would be impressed with her, and I was extremely proud of her—she was twenty-nine-years-old and was going to be the director of the x-ray department. My parents were very proud of her. Her parents wanted to know how much money she was going to make.

I called Chief Sims, and we scheduled an interview the following week. When he offered me the job, he told me he knew I wanted to work in Atmore since that is where we were going to live. He told me he had spoken with the Atmore Chief Gene Bus, and he was expecting a vacancy in three or four months or even sooner. Chief Sims told me when the position came open to give him enough notice to hire a replacement for me. I agreed to do that; I felt like a free agent. I asked if I could ride with an officer on patrol to begin getting familiar with the city, the department, and how the officers worked. He set me up for the following weekend, and I turned in my three-week notice to Mobile that night.

We were on day shift when Billy Mathews and I responded to a call of a suspicious person in Crichton on Springhill Avenue. The caller said the person was acting strange; we saw each other from three blocks away. He walked into the neighborhood and disappeared before I could get to him. Billy and I looked for him for about ten minutes but didn't see him. We got another call about twenty minutes later about the same person who had been spotted several blocks from where we last saw him. Barry saw him from several blocks away, and the guy saw Billy about the same time and walked into the middle of the block. I positioned myself on the east side of the block Billy thought he saw him in while Billy walked through several yards. We never found him. We looked for him in between calls, but we never saw him.

Darrell McMann

A commercial robbery was dispatched as the evening shift was coming on duty. The suspect entered the store armed with a knife, he took a couple of females into a back room, and raped them before leaving with whatever money the store had on hand. Billy called me at home that night and asked me if I heard what happened. I told him I hadn't. He told me about the robbery and what happened to the females. I felt terrible. He said he got a call from a sergeant in investigations, and he asked Billy about the two calls we got. He told Billy he wanted us to write statements. He also said the chief was upset with what happened and wanted some answers. I told him I was more concerned about the victims than how the chief was feeling. We wrote our statements the next day. The suspect was arrested a few days later. We heard the chief was satisfied with what we did, but I didn't really care what he thought.

I rode along with an officer in Brewton the following Saturday night. It was very different. Brewton's shift consisted of a sergeant and two officers covering a city of five thousand people. I worked on a shift with a lieutenant, two sergeants, and ten patrol officers, and we covered a quarter of a city of 205,000 people. Brewton's department had twenty officers while Mobile had 456. The officer I rode with was a newer officer, and I got the feeling she had very little confidence. I was used to being exposed to different types of training and had completed the FTO program before becoming a solo officer. I would discover that departments in most small towns did not have a FTO program. An officer may ride with another officer for a couple of weeks and then become a solo officer.

The shift was quiet for a Saturday night; in Mobile I was usually running from call to call all night. A few hours after the shift began the dispatcher called the sergeant. The victim of a drive-by shooting from a week ago called and said she saw the suspect riding around in his car. He fired several shots at the victim's house the previous week in front of several witnesses. The officer I was riding with told me she knew the car and everyone had dealt with the suspect at least once. We headed to the area and stopped at an intersection with a four-way stop. A car came to a stop heading the opposite direction. She said, "I think that's

Move Along; Nothing to See Here

his car." We eased through the intersection and past his vehicle. She looked at him and said, "Yep, that's him." I thought, "Okay, here we go." She got on the radio and advised that she'd seen him. I was expecting a U-turn, but she continued in the same direction for two blocks and turned. We came to another four-way stop. I couldn't believe the suspect was at this intersection but headed in the opposite direction. We passed each other again as we drove through the intersection. I was expecting a U-turn, but we continued on for another two blocks and turned again. I turned in my seat and watched the suspect drive away. He had to know something was going on by the way she was staring at him. He didn't seem to be very worried. In Mobile we would have been in a car chase or he would have bailed out of the car by now. I told her I had my gun if she wanted to stop him.

We found him again a few minutes later as he was stopping in front of a friend's house. She got on the radio and advised where she was, and she hit her blue lights. The sergeant and the other officer arrived a few seconds later. I was expecting a felony takedown and pulled my gun as I stood behind the passenger door. They walked nonchalantly toward the car. There were four other guys in the car. They stepped out and walked to the back of the house; no one stopped them. They spoke briefly with the suspect and asked if they could search his car. I knew if there had been a gun in the car it was now gone. The passengers walked back to the front yard and watched them search the car. Nothing was found in the vehicle, and the suspect was released. We got back in the car, and she said she was surprised they didn't find any weed in the car. I said, "Yeah, so am I." I was having serious second thoughts about my decision.

We found a nice trailer park about three miles east of Atmore on highway 31 in Canoe for our trailer. The day we moved the trailer, I followed it from Grand Bay to Atmore. I thought it was kind of funny that I was following my house.

Unfortunately, we were now closer to Kim's family. They still didn't come very often. We would have to go see them. Things would really start going downhill soon.

Darrell McMann

One of my last calls in Mobile was on a Sunday morning in Crichton just before 6:00 A.M. A child called and said her mommy and daddy were having problems. It had been a very busy night, but there hadn't been any calls for about two hours, and I was ready to go home. I knocked on the door. An eight-year-old female answered the door; I asked where her parents were. She said they were arguing and were in the back of the house. I followed her through the house, and she pointed to the back of the house and said, "They are in there." She turned and went back to her bedroom.

I walked into the living room and found the parents talking. The female asked me who called. I told her their daughter called because she was worried about them. She said, "Everything is okay." Her husband said, "No, it isn't." He pulled a gun from his back pocket, put it to the side of his head, and started pleading with his wife. I ducked behind the wall and pulled my gun. I got on the radio and advised dispatch about what was happening. Several officers advised they were coming. I talked the female into leaving the room. When she left the room, the husband sat down on the floor and threatened to shoot himself. There was a mirror hanging on the wall, so I could watch him and talk to the female. She told me she caught him cheating on her, and he was pleading his case with her. She told me she could call their pastor, and he could talk to him. Two officers showed up very quickly. I asked them to take the kids out and call the pastor. I peeked around the wall and started talking to the husband. He said he wanted to die and put the gun to his head. I was convinced he was going to shoot himself. He was preparing himself; he got calm. I didn't want to watch someone blow there brains out, but I wasn't going to let him hurt me, so I was ready if he decided he was going to make me do it.

The female all of the sudden walked by me into the room. He stood up, and she reached out to hug him. He stood up and hugged her with one hand. The hand with the gun in it was down to his side, and he was crying. I told one of the officers I was going to get the gun and walked into the room. I grabbed his wrist, and he let go of the gun. I opened the cylinder and found it was empty. He looked at me and said, "I knew it was empty." I felt like shooting him, but I didn't. His

Move Along; Nothing to See Here

pastor lived close by, and I talked to him when he showed up. He said he would counsel them, and I left.

Sgt. Yonkley was waiting on me when I came to the precinct after completing my report. He said, "I heard you on the radio when you said he had a gun to his head. I was walking out of the precinct when I realized I had to take a dump. I knew you could handle it. You gotta have your priorities." I said, "Thanks, Sarge." He asked me if I was still leaving; I told him I was. I hated to leave, but we had already moved to Atmore and it was a great opportunity for Kim. He told me I was a good officer, and he enjoyed working with me. I told him he was a pleasure to work for. I left Mobile in January of 1996

You expect attitude on the street and deal with it. When you get the same attitude from the administration, it's hard to deal with. The department had 456 officers when I completed the FTO program. When I left there were 379.

Chapter 9

When I started with Brewton, my supervisor was Rodney Groves. I liked him, and we talked for a while before our shift started. He introduced me to the other officer on the shift, Junior Simpleton. I didn't care for him very much, and I think the feeling was mutual. I was told later that no one else wanted to work with him, so they put me with him since I was new. We rode together for the first night, and Junior showed me around town. It was a slow night. I asked him where the hot spots were, but he looked at me like I was crazy. Businesses could request an officer to escort employees to the bank to make their deposits. A couple of people rode with us to the bank and back to the business. Junior was proud that he knew when a particular business was close to being ready to go to the bank; I didn't feel it was that important.

We rode together on some nights and at different times on other nights. I didn't know from day to day if we would be riding together or not. I asked officers on other shifts if they rode together. They said no, but Junior liked to sometimes for some unknown reason.

We responded to Kmart one afternoon for a harassment complaint. A female employee was reporting an older male was bothering her at work. He found out what her phone number was and started calling her. She saw him standing in the street in front of her house that morning. I took her information and told her what to do to swear out an arrest warrant. Junior had decided to stay in the cruiser, and when I got back in the cruiser, he noticed my notebook was in my hand. He asked if I was writing a report. I told him I was writing a stalking report. He said, "Stalking? We ain't got shit for stalking!" I said, "What do you mean? You didn't even hear what she said." He said, "I don't have to hear what she said—ain't no law for stalking." I smiled and told him to open the trunk. I retrieved the statute book and turned it to the stalking statute. He said, "Well how about that."

Move Along; Nothing to See Here

Sgt. Groves was hurt in traffic crash on duty and was off for several months. A sergeant would work with us or a reserve or full-time officer would join us. Most of the time it was just Junior and me.

I managed to find one of the dope spots in town without the help of Junior; it wasn't hard to find. We were riding together one night headed north on highway 31 when I looked down East Jackson Street and saw three cars stopped in the middle of the street; there were several black males in the street at the windows of the cars. I asked, "Is that a crack spot?" He said, "That's what I hear." I said, "Let's go back, and see what we can get into." He looked at me and said, "We ain't narcotic officers." I said, "Oh, so we have more important things to do like taking people to the bank?" He said, "Yep, you ain't in Mobile anymore."

A couple nights later, I was alone when I passed through East Jackson and saw a car stopped in the street. The guys in the street saw me coming and walked back into their yards. The car turned unto highway 31, and I stopped it a couple of blocks later. I got on the radio and called in my traffic stop, and I said they were suspicious and there were six people in the car. I looked up the street and saw Junior checking out buildings with his spotlight. He turned south heading toward me. I got everyone's ID and started checking them for warrants. Junior never came to assist me. I watched him go around a building across the street from me. We made eye contact, but he continued checking buildings. I asked him later why he didn't back me up. He said, "It was time to check buildings." I was so mad I couldn't think.

A couple of nights later, I was in the Tom Thumb on highway 31 heating up a cheeseburger at 3:00 A.M., when I heard tires screeching. Going over to the window, I watched a pickup truck come to a stop in two parking spaces in front of the store. The driver stumbled out and walked into the store obviously very drunk. She walked up to me and said, "You know Paul Biddle?" I told her I didn't know him. She said, "Yeah, you know Paul Biddle. EVERYONE knows Paul Biddle!" I said, "I DO NOT know the man!" She said, "Yes, you do." I said, "Okay, I forgot, I know him." She said, "I takes care of him." I said, "That's great. Maybe he can pick you up." She said, "WHY? I ain't drunk. You ain't goin' to rest me are ya?" I said, "If you get back in that truck I will put you in jail." She said, "You couldn't catch me." I jokingly said, "If you beat me to the house, I won't put you in jail." I turned around when the microwave dinged.

I heard the jingle when the door opened, and the cashier said, "There she goes." I looked and the drunk was backing up and almost hit the gas pumps. She took off out of the parking lot headed north on 31. I jumped in the cruiser and took off after her. She was going pretty fast, but I saw her make a right turn just before leaving the city limits. There were no streetlights and no houses along the stretch of road we were on. I was going around eighty and thought I had lost her when I saw her brake lights when she reached an intersection— she was driving with her lights out. She ran that stop sign and the next one. I caught up to her as she was pulling into the driveway. I grabbed her as she was walking up to the front door and arrested her. She said, "I takes care of Paul!" I said, "That's wonderful. Maybe he can pay your bond." She told me I was in deep trouble. I wondered aloud how concerned I was.

Two rednecks from East Brewton kidnapped an elderly man at gunpoint from his house late one night. The tied him up, threw him in the trunk of their car, and left town. They stopped at the BP at highway 31 and highway 113 in Flomaton to buy beer. The old man escaped while they were in the store. They didn't count on him escaping because he knew who they were.

Two days later Candy Clark and I were riding together. We were sitting in the cruiser at TR Miller High School watching a baseball game. Junior called me on the radio and asked me to switch to code, which supposedly blocked the radio transmission from being heard on scanners. I could barely understand what was said when we used it. Junior asked me where we were. I told him we were at TR Miller. He told me to come to the police department and drop Candy off. He said she could get a car to cover the city while we were busy. I asked him what was going on. He said, "Did you hear about that thing?"

Move Along; Nothing to See Here

I said, "What thing?" He said, "The thing in Flomaton." I said, "What thing in Flomaton?" He said, "You know the thing in Flomaton." I said, "Oh, that thing." I looked at Candy, and we both shook our heads. He called me two more times as we were on our way; each time he wanted to know where I was and each time he had me switch to code again.

He said, "We need to meet the East Brewton lieutenant in East Brewton." I thought, "Somehow that makes sense." He told me where he would be waiting in East Brewton for me just across the city limits. I said to Candy, "He sounds excited. This should be interesting, but I wish I knew what he was talking about." We laughed. I dropped Candy off and crossed the bridge into East Brewton. I saw Junior waiting on the side of the road. He took off, and I followed.

We made a couple of turns and drove around the block at about sixty miles per hour. We drove around the block again; I stopped and waited as Junior drove around the block a third time. He looked surprised to see me waiting on him. He stopped next to me, and I said, "Would you mind telling me why we are racing around the block like a couple of idiots!" He said, "We are meeting the East Brewton lieutenant at the house of the suspect that took that old man." I asked him which house, but he didn't know and then he said, "There's the lieutenant," and we took off again.

We went to a house in the middle of the block that I had driven by twice and Junior, three times; I found the back door open. There were two cold beers sitting on the kitchen table and a cigarette burning in the ashtray. Junior said, "Looks like they left." I said, "Really, I never would have thought it. I can't imagine how they would have realized we were coming."

Chief Mack called me the following Monday for an interview with Chief Bus in Atmore. Chief Sims had several applicants to choose from and hired someone within a few days. I submitted my notice a couple days after my interview and became an officer in Atmore in May of 1996. Junior and I only spoke when it was necessary when we worked.

Chapter 10

Atmore is a city of just over 8,000 people. The police department had twenty-four officers at the time and worked twelve-hour shifts that changed from nights to days every two weeks. A shift consisted of a sergeant and three officers; I discovered right away that Atmore was much busier than Brewton.

One of the first calls I responded to was for a disturbance at the park on MLK. We cleared the parking lot, and as I turned around to walk back to my cruiser, I noticed Dan Leak was talking with two guys on the other side of the parking lot. I noticed they were looking at me. When I got closer I heard Dan ask them, "Is that him?" One of them said, "Yeah, that's him." Dan said, "They recognized you from all the way over there. They are from Mobile." The guy said, "We live in Toulminville, and we used to see you all the time. Ain't you Baby Adams?" We talked about the good old days for a couple of minutes.

Atmore had somewhat of a gang problem; four young guys across the tracks called themselves the Four Horsemen. They could have been more of a problem, but they weren't very bright. They didn't adopt any national gang's tendencies except for the Blood's style of graffiti.

We responded to a disturbance one night called in by the next door neighbors; I was the first officer on the scene. As I walked toward the house, I contacted a female in the driveway covered in blood from a head wound. She said, "It's my husband—he has a gun." I pulled my gun and led her down the street to meet the ambulance. Two other officers entered the house and found the husband sitting in the living room. They recovered a sawed off shotgun and a small-caliber handgun. He had become addicted to crystal methamphetamine and left; she had not heard from him in over six months. A coworker asked her to go out to dinner and have a few drinks. The husband was hiding in

Move Along; Nothing to See Here

the backyard waiting for her to come home. When they got out of the car, he ran up to her date and put the shotgun to his head. He pulled the trigger, but the gun misfired. He pointed the handgun at him and told him to take his clothes off. When he did, he told him to run; we found him several blocks away hiding in the bushes. The husband had put the handgun to her heard and pulled the trigger, but it misfired, too. He got mad and hit her several times with the butt of the shotgun.

Bruce Moss and I arrested a drunken white guy causing a disturbance in the middle of the street; he was very obnoxious. As we were walking in the police department, he was yelling, "Whatever you do you better not put me in a cell with a bunch of niggers!" We processed him and were about to put him in a cell when he saw Larry Hart, a black officer. He said, "Oh that's just great. Ya'll got them uniform too!" Larry asked him what he meant by *them*. I closed my eyes when the drunk said, "NIGGERS! NIGGERS in uniform. NIGGERS out of uniform." Larry laughed and walked away.

We took him into the male cell area and realized we had ten prisoners, and they were all black males. They had heard everything he said. One of the guys, who had spent about fifteen years in prison, looked at me, smiled, and said, "McMann, why don't you put him in here with me. I will take care of him." I wanted to but knew something bad would happen. We decided to put him in the women's cell area since we didn't have any female prisoners. We put him in the cell, and he said, "Yeah, I would have to kill me a few niggers if you left me in there."

I reported for work the next day and heard one of the prisoners say, "Officer McMann, could you come back here, please?" I walked back and found Mr. Obnoxious had been moved to the male side of our little jail. He said, "I would like to apologize for my behavior last night." I smiled and looked at his cell mate who was reclining on the bed. He winked at me and smiled. I said, "I accept your apology, but you used some very racist comments last night toward your new friends and Officer Hart." He cleared his throat and said, 'I know, and

Darrell McMann

I apologized." I asked, "Did your new friends express their displeasure with the comments you made?" He nodded his head yes. He hadn't been hurt, but they must have had an interesting conversation. Larry walked by, and I asked him to come in. I told him that Mr. Obnoxious wanted to apologize at the behest of his new friends. Larry laughed and walked away.

Rusty Clark and I responded to a disturbance near a hotel. I turned the corner and saw a car in the parking lot with the driver side door ajar, but I didn't see anyone. I stopped and approached the car to check it out. I looked inside and saw that no one was inside and didn't see anything incriminating. I heard Rusty say, "Hey, I got someone here." A black male wearing all black had been stabbed in the chest with a screwdriver and was lying on the side of the road next to the entrance of the parking lot. I realized I had come close to running over him. Rusty started CPR, and I called for an ambulance; he died on the way to the hospital. Some witnesses came forward a few minutes later and told us who stabbed him.

Word travels fast in a small town especially in the black community. Someone called the police department and told the dispatcher the suspect was just seen close to the Patterson Street projects. The sergeant sent me to see if I could find anyone who had seen him. I parked and got out of my cruiser. Two guys walked over to me; they looked around and told me they had just walked through the vacant lot across the street from where we were standing. One guy told me he was walking through the trees when someone asked him if he could get a smoke from him. He gave him a cigarette and noticed he had blood on him. The suspect told him not to tell anyone he was in there. The sergeant joined me as the guy was telling me the story.

Dispatch called the sergeant and told him someone may have seen the suspect a few blocks north of Patterson Street. He sent Cory Brewer to check out the latest sighting. A few seconds later, we heard a gunshot not to far away. The sergeant told me to get on the north side of the vacant lot. He said he was thinking about calling the tracking dogs at Fountain Prison just north of town. As I turned the corner, I saw several people in the middle of the street fighting. I pulled up, and they yelled, "This is the nigger that killed my home-boy!" They threw him on my cruiser; I cuffed him and put him in the backseat. When I turned around, they had walked away.

Kim would make lunch for me when I worked days on the weekends if she was home. She called me one Saturday afternoon and told me lunch was ready. As I turned into the driveway, I noticed a pickup truck leaving the park and heading toward town. I noticed Kim and Elizabeth were standing outside waiting on me. Kim motioned for me to stop next to her. When I stopped, she said, "The guy driving that truck was staring at one of us, but I'm not sure which one of us he was staring at." Elizabeth was three-years-old at the time. I turned around and caught up to the truck halfway back to town.

I approached the truck and said, "Hey, I'm stopping you because I got a complaint you were acting suspiciously back there in the trailer park. What were you doing there if you don't mind me asking?" He said, "I was waiting for my niece to come home." I asked him which trailer she lived in and what was her name." He said, "Her name is Kathy, and she lives in the blue trailer in the front." I said, "I don't think you are being honest with me. Did you see the lady and the little girl in front of the beige trailer?" He nodded yes. I said, "I live in the beige trailer and that was my wife and daughter standing outside. I know the people next door in the blue trailer. The female that lives there doesn't go by that name. Her husband is a dispatcher who happens to be working now. I'm not going to ask you who you were staring at because I don't think I really want to know.

I asked for his driver's license and took down all his information. He lived just south of Bay Minette in Baldwin County. I said, "I am going to call Bay Minette PD and check to see if they know you. I am going to call the Baldwin County Sheriff's Office also. I'm sure between those two agencies at least one of them is going to be familiar with you. I don't want to see you around here ever again." He said, "You won't." He happened to be a prior sexual offender but wasn't on probation at the time. I never saw him again.

Darrell McMann

We responded to one of the bars in town for a disturbance. A married couple was very drunk and arguing with each other and everyone else. The bartender wanted them to leave; we asked them to go outside to decide what we were going to do. The husband opened the door to walk out and was punched in the back of his head by his wife. She kicked his backside as he stumbled, and he fell to the ground. She put up a brief fight while we tried to cuff her. The husband didn't want her to go to jail and grabbed me from behind; he went to jail too.

We put them in the cells and started the paperwork. The female was screaming at the top of her lungs. Chief Mack asked me what she was screaming at. I told him I didn't know and that she was drunk. He asked me to go back, talk to her, and try to calm her down; I walked into the cell area. As I turned the corner and was about to stand in front of the cell, I was nearly hit with something she had thrown—it was a white glob of toilet paper soaked with blood. I looked in the cell. She had a roll of toilet paper in one hand and a large wad in the other; her panties were down to her knees. She said, "I'm on my period you bastard! I need some tampons!" I found the chief and told him. He handed me $5 and asked me to go to Winn Dixie and get some. I brought them back and told her I had tampons for her. She said, "It's about time you bastard." I told her she was welcome and left.

One evening, I was on Main Street when I noticed that a small, red truck in front of me was weaving. I followed it for a few minutes and noted the driving pattern. I pulled the truck over and contacted the driver who looked like Captain Caveman. He told me he just got off work and hadn't been drinking. I said, "I didn't ask you if you had been drinking. But now that you mention it, I noticed you were weaving." He said, "No, I don't think so." I asked him why his eyes were bloodshot and his speech was slurred. He said, "I'm tired. It's been long day." I asked him why his breath smelled of alcohol. He said, "I've been sick, and I just had some cough syrup." I said, "So, you haven't had anything to drink." He said, "No." I asked, "Is that a Budweiser you have stuck between your legs?" He said, "I dip Skoal, and I use it as a spit cup." I asked him to hand me the can. He did. It was cold and half full of Budweiser.

Move Along; Nothing to See Here

I asked him if he would get out and take a few sobriety tests for me. He said, "Okay," and almost fell when he stepped out. He couldn't do anything I asked and couldn't follow directions. I told him he was under arrest. He said, "I'm just going home, and your messing with me." I told him he needed to turn around and put his hands behind his back or I would help him. He threw a punch at me, missed, lost his balance, and fell to the ground; I cuffed him.

Two months later I saw him again. I knew his license was suspended and decided to follow him to get a driving pattern in case he was drunk again. I noticed he was weaving. He ran a stop sign when he was paying to much attention to me. I turned my overhead lights on, and he stopped. He got out of the truck, stumbling badly, and met me halfway between the vehicles. Before I could say anything, he told me he wasn't drunk and was just going home. I noticed he tensed up and assumed a fighting stance. I gave him a quick shot to the forehead with my palm, knocking him down. I jumped on top of him and cuffed him. He refused to take a breath test for the second time.

About four months later, I saw Captain Caveman in his little red truck. I followed him again to get a driving pattern. He immediately stops and jumps out of his truck and meets me halfway. Before I can say anything, he tries to sneak a punch but misses. He darts to his right to run away on foot but forgot there was a six-foot ditch that was half full of water from a recent heavy rain. He fell in, and I started laughing. He looked up at me and said, "You better help me out of here, or I am going to kick your ass!" I said, "Looks like I have a fight on my hands because I ain't getting wet and muddy. Either way you are going to jail." He climbed out, and I cuffed him.

I responded to the scene of a shooting on Carver Avenue one afternoon. I found the victim lying on the side of the street with a couple of bullet wounds and a shotgun lying next to him. His brother showed up just after I did. His brother begged me to do something for him, but I couldn't. He was still breathing and wasn't bleeding very badly. I could tell he had been shot at least three times with a small caliber handgun. A small caliber round is deadly to internal organs.

Darrell McMann

The round ricochets inside the body causing lots of damage. The ambulance was there within minutes, but he didn't make it.

The next day I was sitting in our break room eating lunch when Dan Leak walked in with a black male. He told him to have a seat and left the room. I didn't know he was the homicide suspect, so I said, "What's up man?" He said, "Do you think I could claim self-defense?" I wasn't sure what he was talking about and was about to ask him when Dan came back to get him. The sergeant said, "That's our shooter from yesterday." I said, "It would have been nice to know that since I'm in here eating lunch and not knowing I'm sitting next to a homicide suspect."

The suspect and the victim were having an ongoing dispute. They had threatened each other, and they both started carrying guns. The suspect happened to walk by the victim's girlfriend's house. The victim grabbed a shotgun and ran out to shoot the suspect. He only had two shells, and he missed both shots. The suspect was carrying a .380. He emptied the magazine hitting the victim three times in the chest.

A female called 911 one night, screaming her ex-husband was trying to break in her house. She gave a description of him and his car, we were there within two minutes. She was extremely scared and worried that he would come back. She told me he was trying to pry the back door open, but I didn't see any evidence of that. We were close enough to the house to see someone leaving in a car when she said he left, and we didn't see a vehicle leaving the area. She also said he stood at her window trying to get it open, but I didn't see any footprints in the dirt beneath window or any marks on the windows. I told her I would write a report, and she could obtain a copy. I told her to call us back if she thought she needed to.

She called 911 again about ten minutes later and told the dispatcher he was trying to break down the door; his car was parked in the street in front of her house. I was about three blocks away and was there within thirty seconds. I didn't see a car in the street and found no evidence of him trying to pry the front door open. I told her

Move Along; Nothing to See Here

I would add that to the report and to contact her attorney. She should go to court and apply for an Order for Protection. She told me thank you and closed the door. I called dispatch and advised I was going to park down the street and watch her house. I turned the lights off and shut the cruiser down. I also advised dispatch not to let the female know I was down the street if she called again.

She called 911 within fifteen minutes and told the dispatcher her ex-husband was trying to break in again. I told the dispatcher to ask her if he had parked his car in the street again or had come back on foot. She said the car was parked in the middle of the street with the headlights on. I could plainly see there were no vehicles in the street. I got out of my cruiser and walked toward her house; I asked where he was. She told the dispatcher he just tried to break down the front door and was now standing in the front yard with a gun in his hand. I was standing behind a tree in the neighbors' yard watching her talk on the phone on her front porch. Then she said that he just fired a couple of rounds into the house. She was facing the other direction when I contacted her; she was very surprised to see me. I pointed to my cruiser down the street and said, "I've been right there since I left your house. Nothing has happened." She walked in the house and closed the door.

One of the night shift dispatchers was, for lack of a more aptly descriptive word, a mess. She was very sweet. If she got a serious 911 call, we had to decipher it from her over the radio. Our call numbers were three digit numbers that started with 401 and ended at 429. She would come on the radio and say, " Fo UUUUHHH Fo ARUHH-HAAAUU!" One of us would say, "Just tell us where it is and what it is." Usually we would just get the location and sort it out from there. She brought buckets of unshelled peas and would spend the night shucking peas. She would play gospel music very loud and mop the floors, which wasn't one of her duties. She would call one of us to come to the police department because the prisoners were yelling at her. We turned the music down which would make the prisoners happy, and they would go back to sleep. One of my fellow officers

Darrell McMann

called her one night at about 3:00 A.M. on a week day on the main line. He disguised his voice and told her he was down by the high school and was watching a strange light hovering over the park. She started to panic, and we heard her breathing on the radio. He told her to hold on that something is happening, and then he hung up. He called her back yelling frantically a few minutes later and told her something has landed in the park and that dust and smoke were everywhere. She said, "OH, LAWDY JESUS! I GOTS TO CALL SOMEBODY!" He told her something was happening and hung up. We heard her breathing on the radio again. He called back a few minutes later. He was whispering when he said, "I think something or someone is getting off the thing. I gotta get outta here before they see me. GET SOME HELP!!" He hung up. We heard her breathing again on the radio, as she said, "Fo uh Fo uuuu Fo, OH LAWD!!!"

We were laughing too hard to get on the radio and ask her what was going on. She gave up on trying to dispatch us. We got ourselves together and asked her if she had a call. She said, "Lights at the high school!" I asked, "The lights are on at the high school?" She said, "NO LIGHTS AT THE PARK BY THE HIGH SCHOOL!" I said, "We turned them off earlier." She said, "NO LIGHTS IN THE SKY!" I said, "Are talking about stars?" She said, "OH LAWD NEVERMIND!"

Kim and I purchased a small blow up swimming pool and took it to her parents' house in the summer of 1997 for Elizabeth and our niece to play in. Our niece was around a year older than Elizabeth. I put on some shorts and got in it to play with them. The girls and I were having a blast. My niece stood up, and I noticed her swimsuit was sagging. I said, "Hey girl, you are about to come out of your suit." She laughed and jumped on top of me.

Kim's sister called later that night. She told Kim that their mom was upset with me. Their mom declared that I was a child molester and was no longer welcome on her property. Kim said, "Why would she say that? We were all right there. Nothing happened and nothing like that would ever happen." Her sister said, "That's just Mom."

Move Along; Nothing to See Here

Kim told me what her mother said. I said, "Fine I won't go back up there." Her mother called a few months later; I answered the phone. She said, "Why haven't you been up here lately? You must have to work a lot." I said, "Yeah, that's it." I handed the phone to Kim. I wanted to have it out with her, but Kim was afraid it would just get worse; I agreed to keep my mouth shut.

Kim and I met her parents and her sister at the flea market in Mobile a couple of weeks after her mother made the child molester comment. I didn't want to go, but Kim talked me into to it. I started flirting innocently with Kim's sister. Kim was laughing along with her parents and was egging it on. We found out later her mother didn't think it was very funny and accused me of trying to get into her pants. That was pretty much the end of it for me.

The mayoral race in 1998 was hotly contested. The black community felt the mayor, Howard Small, didn't care about their issues. Ricky Oden, a chiropractor in town, was running against Small. He sought out the residents' input and was making some people excited and some people antsy; I didn't care. I thought he was just another politician trying to get himself elected. He had the ear of the city employees, especially the police and fire departments because he promised to increase funding and raise our salaries.

The city employees were disappointed when they realized the new mayor wasn't going to do as he promised. His popularity plummeted and morale, especially at the police department, dropped so low most of us hated coming to work. It got so bad the mayor and chief called a departmental meeting. They had the sheriff's office come and take calls so the whole department could attend.

The mayor wanted to know what he could do to make things better; several us of told him. He didn't seem to like what we told him. One of the officers became disgusted and said, "I don't know why you called this meeting. You don't care, and you lied to us. Nothing is going to change." The mayor sweet talked him and asked him to give him a chance to make it right. We ended up getting a little raise but

Darrell McMann

nothing like he had promised. I was only there for about half of his term. Carl Prim conducted a little research and found that sixty-two officers came and left during his term. That's amazing considering the PD has only twenty-six officers.

Larry and I responded to a suspicious circumstances complaint on Patterson Street just before lunch. The property manager met us at one of the apartments. He told us no one had heard from or seen the elderly man who lived in the apartment. He showed me some fluid covered with maggots that had seeped through the wall to the outside of the house. I could see flies covering the windows and could barely make out the unmistakable odor of rotting flesh. I asked Larry if he had ever experienced a death since he had become an officer. He said, "How do you know someone in there is dead?" I showed him the fluid, the maggots, and the flies. The property manager gave me a spare key to the apartment. I noticed Larry was standing on the sidewalk about three feet from the front door. I said, "I'm going to open the door and move over there." I pointed to a spot twenty feet away. I said, "You need to move, you don't want to be there, the fumes will get you." He either didn't here me, or he was too excited about what was happening. I opened the door and moved to the spot I had indicated, but Larry didn't move. The fumes hit him, and he vomited; I grabbed him and took him to fresh air. I covered my nose with my T-shirt and peeked in. Thankfully the deceased was only a couple feet from the door and was obviously dead. Later, Larry said, "Next time, I'll know because I still have the smell in my nose." I told him to go home and wash his uniform.

Larry and I responded to Winn Dixie for a shoplifting complaint. We contacted the manager, who told us the suspect was trying to return an item without a receipt, and he believed the suspect or someone else had stolen it. The manager didn't want him arrested but wanted him to leave. The suspect didn't understand why Winn Dixie wouldn't give him a refund and was getting very belligerent. We told him we couldn't force Winn Dixie to give him a refund, and he needed to leave. He walked outside and began cursing loudly as he walked out to his car in front of several children. I said, "You need to

Move Along; Nothing to See Here

watch your mouth or your going to jail!" He turned around, extended his middle finger, and yelled, "KISS MY ASS!" I said, "Stop, your under arrest!" He took off on foot.

Larry and I chased him through the neighborhood and into the front yard of a house. He stood in the yard and dared us to come get him. We took a few steps toward him, and he took off again on foot. Jeff Bradley pulled up behind him, and he turned to face him. I had had enough. I was about twenty yards from him and charged him while his attention was focused on Jeff. He heard me coming, but it was too late. He turned as I tackled him. We hit the ground with me on the bottom, which isn't a good place to be. He was about to punch me when I grabbed a handful of groin and told him I would rip off everything the good Lord gave him. Larry and Jeff cuffed him, and we were met at the jail by his parents who were screaming and yelling about how we abused their baby boy, and we were nothing but racists. The chief took them in his office and was able to calm them down. They were threatening to sue us for police brutality. I laughed and that made them really irate. I had to go to the hospital when I realized I could barely walk. My holster was forced into my hip when I landed on top of a root of a tree. I was sore for a couple days.

I was in the police department one afternoon when the dispatcher asked me to relieve her so she could use the bathroom. I answered a 911 call. The caller was a child who said her daddy was beating up her mommy. I got the address and a description of her daddy as the dispatcher came back. I could hear a disturbance in the background and what sounded like someone being slapped. I walked out and told her where I was going.

The wife and the kids were in the front yard when I got there. They were all crying and hysterical. She had handprints on her neck from being choked, her nose and bottom lip were bleeding, and her face was discolored. I also noticed it looked like her hair had been pulled. I walked in the house and found the husband in the kitchen. He said, "Well, I guess I gotta go." I said, "That's right, you're under arrest. Turn around." I cuffed him and led him out to the cruiser.

Darrell McMann

On the way to the jail he asked me, "I can make a phone call, right?" I said, "Yes, you can." He said, "I can call anyone I want?" I said, "Yes, you can call anyone you want." I looked in the rearview mirror and noticed he was smiling. We got to the police department, and he asked me when he could make his phone call. I told him just as soon as I completed the booking process and fingerprinted him. When I finished, I pointed at the phone and told him he could make his call. He smiled. I heard him pick up the phone and then he said, "Is Don home?" When "Don" got on the phone, he told him he was in jail. The suspect said, "Excuse me, the chief wants to speak to you." He had a big smile when he handed me the phone. The chief asked me what was going on, and I told him the story. He said, "Looks like he's going to have to get comfortable." I said, "Yes sir."

I sat down and finished the form I was working on. The suspect said, "So what did Don say?" I said, "He said for you to get comfortable." I said, "He can't do anything for you when it's domestic violence. You don't get a bond for a minimum of twenty-four hours." He screamed, "WHY?" I said, "The state of Alabama passed legislation that leaves officers very little discretion when they investigate a domestic violence incident. We are mandated by law to make an arrest." He said, "I guess I should have called a lawyer." I didn't tell him I could let him make another call. He didn't ask, so I didn't tell him.

Jed Wilkins was city councilman in Atmore who lived two houses down from a very active crack house and was a vocal critic of the police department. If I lived near a crack house I would complain, too. I started working Elbert's house pretty hard. Elbert owned the house but didn't pay any bills. He didn't have power or water. He didn't have a driveway, but there was so much traffic that the vehicles had created a path completely around his house. I decided not to be sneaky and decided to use the direct approach. I would park in front of his house and talk to whoever was there. I knew I would be lucky to get any dope because they could see me coming from several blocks away. I found a pathway through the backyards between the side streets and walked up on a few people going to or coming from Elbert's. I caught a few people using. I told Elbert, people were worried about him, which was why I was checking on him so frequently. I asked Elbert if he minded if I parked in his driveway or in his backyard. He told me he didn't mind, but I don't think he actually thought I was going to do it.

One night I parked about two blocks away from Elbert's at an intersection. An officer from the Poarch Creek Reservation pulled up next to me, and we talked for a few minutes. I didn't see the car that stopped at Elbert's. The Poarch officer left a few minutes later to return to the reservation. About five minutes later, I heard several gunshots and then a car went by me at high speed. I got on the radio and notified everyone what was happening as I was catching up to the car. I hit my lights for him to stop, but he accelerated to around ninety miles per hour as we headed south down MLK. The driver turned east on highway 31 and then into the parking lot of a motel. He got out of the car and was about to open the door to go into a room when I grabbed him from behind. I noticed there was blood on the side of his head. I turned him around and saw he had been shot with a small caliber gun in his forehead. He was in shock and didn't realize I was trying to stop him. I called him an ambulance. The bullet had come to a rest next to his ear just under the skin. He was shot by a "friend" over a drug deal gone bad. Elbert was a reluctant witness.

I was in the police department one afternoon when a female came in with her parents and children. She was afraid of her husband. He had been using crystal meth for three months and had hit her several times. He threatened to kill her, the children, and her parents. She had several bruises on her back, arms, legs, and face. They lived outside of town, so I told them I would have a county deputy come to the police department. I went back to the lobby and told them a deputy would be coming in a few minutes. Her dad stood up and walked over to me. He was in his mid-sixties and about five-feet-six but looked like he could bench press a car. He said, "If he hurts my baby again, I am going to shoot him." He looked serious and angry, so I decided not lecture him. I said, 'Well hopefully, you won't have to do that." He sat down.

Darrell McMann

A couple weeks later, the sheriff's dispatch called and asked if we could go to Nokomis for a report of shots fired. The sergeant told to me to go.

When I pulled up in the yard I saw the old man, and another guy I knew who was a good friend of one of the officers on the department. I said, "What's going on?" The old man pointed to the backyard. I looked and saw his son-in-law lying on the ground. I could see he had been shot in the chest. I knew he wasn't going to make it. He was barely breathing, and he barely had a pulse. I called dispatch and told them I needed an ambulance. I also told her to advise the county they had a shooting.

I walked back over to the old man and asked if he heard anything. He said, "I told him to stay away from my baby." I said, "Did he hit your daughter again?" He said, "Yes, I told him I was going to shoot him and I did." I looked down and noticed a bulge in his front pocket. I said, "I need you to put your hands behind your head, and I am going to get the gun out of your pocket." He said, "The gun is mine." I said, "I know it's your gun. I just want to make sure no one else gets hurt. You will get it back." He said, "It's my gun, and ain't nobody takin' my gun!" He put his hand in his pocket and started pulling it out. I grabbed his wrist and said, "I know you are upset, but I just have to put the gun somewhere safe. I know what's been going on, and you aren't under arrest. I just want to get the gun." He said, "You ain't getting it!" I forced him onto the hood of my cruiser on his back while holding his wrist.

He was wearing cowboy boots, and I noticed he had drawn his leg back. He kicked me in the middle of my forehead, and I saw stars for a second and got extremely pissed. I raised my flashlight to work on him a little when the friend said, "Hey, Darrell! Let me help you!" I didn't really want to hit an old man with my flashlight, so I said, "You hold his arms while I get the gun. He grabbed his arms, and I got the gun out of his pocket and threw it on the front seat of my cruiser. I cuffed the old man and put him in the backseat.

Move Along; Nothing to See Here

The friend said, "I thought you said he wasn't under arrest." I said, "He isn't. I'm detaining him. He kicked me in the head once already, so I'm not in the mood to see if he is going to do it again." He said "Oh, Okay."

The investigator looked at the imprint on my forehead and asked if I wanted him charged for kicking me and resisting arrest; I told him no. The old man apologized to me on the way to sheriff's substation. He wasn't apologizing, hoping I wouldn't arrest him for it. He realized what he had done and knew I didn't deserve what he did to me. I accepted his apology, and I told him we wouldn't worry about it anymore. The district attorney presented the case before a grand jury. They found the shooting was justified.

Chapter 11

One of the sergeants I worked for took incompetence to a level never seen before. He not only took it to a new level, but he put a face on it for me. I didn't like anything about Al Sharpton. When I first met him he had a front tooth that was loose. When he would speak, I mean grunt, the tooth would move back and forth. I was expecting it to fly out suddenly with a large sample of saliva and put someone's eye out. He eventually had it pulled. He was too lazy to speak coherently, and while I could understand what he was saying most of the time, I would act like I couldn't. He would eventually gather his thoughts and speak more slowly so you could understand what he was saying.

It was obvious from the beginning that I didn't think much of Al. I worked with two officers, Carl Prim and Pete Head, who were very good officers; we became friends. I was generally embarrassed that Al wore a uniform. He would go to the bus station for breakfast when we worked the night shift and fall asleep at the counter. He walked into the police department with scrambled eggs hanging off of his badge.

We all responded to a disturbance one night across the tracks. We found a male chasing a female. We questioned them briefly, and Al told Carl and Pete to take the male to the hospital to get treated for a laceration on his head. Al told me to take the female to the station and charge her with domestic violence felony. I said, "Shouldn't we try and determine what happened?" He ignored me and left.

The female told me her brother was drunk and was yelling at her children; she told him to quit yelling at them. He picked up a vase and struck the side of her head, knocking her unconscious. She had a large knot above her ear and appeared to be in pain. She told me when she woke up; he was chasing the kids around the house with a knife. She picked up a bat and hit him on the back of his head. We entered the fray a few minutes later. I talked to Carl on the phone; we came to the conclusion she was telling the truth.

Move Along; Nothing to See Here

Since Al wanted me to arrest her I told her I would swear out a warrant later if I couldn't convince Al otherwise. I told her she may need to go to the hospital, and I called someone to pick her up.

Al came to the police department and asked me where my prisoner was. I told him I let her go. He asked why; I told him what we learned. He said, "I wanted her charged with domestic violence!" I said, "Domestic violence isn't a charge, it's an act of the legislature. It enhances the penalties of crimes committed that fall into the legal description of domestic violence." He said, "Yeah, but he was bleeding!" I said, "It doesn't matter, you can protect yourself or others from bodily harm. That is what she was doing, and she was hurt too." He said, "I don't care. I want her charged." I said, "If you want her, you go get her." I walked out. He didn't go get her.

Al's philosophy of supervising annoyed me to no end. He would have another officer or dispatcher pass information to me. I walked into dispatch one night, and the dispatcher informed me that Al was upset about something and had told the dispatcher what he wanted me to know. I called Al and asked him to meet me at the back of the police department. When he pulled in, I walked up to his window and asked him if he had a problem with me. He said, "No, but I think you have a problem with me!" I said, "Yes, I do. I have a problem with you supervising me through someone else. If you want me to know something, you need to tell me not someone else." He said, "You want to go to another shift?" I said, "No, you just need to supervise me yourself and not by committee." He said, "I don't think you respect me." I said, "I don't." He looked at me for about thirty seconds and drove away.

I would go out of my way to annoy him. When we worked days on the weekends I would go to the police department several times a day and sit with the dispatcher. He would park in front of the police department and watch me. The dispatcher can be seen from the parking lot. He would get tired of watching me and leave. I would leave and work traffic for a few hours. I would come back and turn in my tickets. I came back one afternoon and noticed the extra chair was gone. I asked the dispatcher where the chair was. She told me Al

Darrell McMann

took it out. I looked out and noticed he was watching me again from the parking lot. I stepped into our break room and got another chair.

One night Al was sent to a car crash on the state line; the dispatcher told him she didn't know if the crash was in Alabama or Florida. The Florida Highway Patrol was on the way too. Al showed up and saw the vehicle in the ditch in Florida. He didn't get out of his cruiser and left when the ambulance arrived. About thirty minutes later the dispatcher called and told me the Florida Highway Patrol Trooper wanted one of us to contact him. When I got there the trooper said, "Hey, I don't know which officer came earlier, but I need to show you something." I said, "Okay." The trooper pointed out some fresh skid marks on the Alabama side of the state line and the point of impact in the ditch was also in Alabama. The car had flipped several times and came to a rest in Florida. The trooper said, "The witnesses told me the Atmore officer never got out of his car. According to the witnesses, the driver appeared to be drunk, and there wasn't anything in the road to cause him to leave the roadway. I'm not trying to pass this off on anyone, but I thought someone should know." I said, "I don't know what happened either, but I will work it." He said, "Okay," and left.

I spoke to the witnesses who thankfully had stuck around. They asked what was wrong with the first officer who showed up; I told them I didn't know. It's embarrassing to admit to a citizen you work for an incompetent moron. I contacted the driver at the hospital who was obviously drunk. He told me a car heading north came into his lane forcing him off the road. I told him several cars were behind him and didn't see a vehicle come into the lane. He told me they were lying. I said, "Okay," and asked the hospital to draw blood for my investigation. The driver was injured and most likely would be in the hospital for a few days.

I finished my report and went to the police department. I walked in and found Al talking to two deputies. I handed him my report. He said, "What's this?" I said, "It's a crash report." He said, "They gonna send this back." I said, "Why is they gonna send it back?" He laughed and said, "Because it happened in Florida. Didn't you see the state line

Move Along; Nothing to See Here

sign?" Needless to say I was a tiny bit pissed. I said, "YEAH, I saw the sign! I also saw the skid marks in Alabama and the point of impact in Alabama. The car flipped into Florida. If you would have done your job and got your lazy self out of the car, I wouldn't have had to go behind you and do it. I was also asked what was wrong with the first officer. By the way, the driver is drunk, and the hospital is drawing blood for me. You still think they gonna send it back?" He said, "I guess not."

After leaving the park on the north side of town for a disturbance, Al decided to share with us on the radio his philosophy concerning traffic jams. He explained his position on the subject—at least that's what I'm assuming because I couldn't understand what he was saying. "It's called a bottle jam," he said. I said, "What was that?" He said, "A bottle jam." I said, "A bottle of jam?' He said, a little annoyed, "NO! A bottle jam." I said, "Don't you mean a bottleneck?" He said, "Oh yeah, you're right. It's a bottleneck."

The employer of a young man on work release called the sheriff's office and told them he had to fire him because he couldn't follow directions. The guy got mad and told him he would be back later; he was going to go home get a gun and kill him. The guy's family lived in Atmore. We were familiar with him because of his criminal tendencies. The sheriff's office advised us someone picked him up; he could be armed.

I spotted him as he got out of a car on the side of highway 21 about three blocks from his family's house. He was carrying his T-shirt in a way that suggested he was hiding something in it. Al was behind me. The guy took off running with us behind him; Al went around me and cut him off at the next street. He turned and ran into a wooded lot; I ran in behind him, drew my gun, and ordered him to stop. He stopped but kept his hands wrapped around his T-shirt while facing away from me. I ordered him to slowly show me his hands and drop to his knees. He told me he had nothing to live for and started walking away. I ran up behind him, grabbed the back of his neck, and forced him to the ground. I put my gun behind his ear and told him

Darrell McMann

to give up. He decided I was serious and had the upper hand, so he gave up. He didn't have anything in his T-shirt; he said he was hoping I would shoot him. I walked him out to my cruiser and noticed Al was nowhere in sight. I got to the police department and found Al talking about how we got the guy. I said, "What's this *WE* shit! Where were you?" He walked out.

I responded to the Days Inn a couple of days later in reference to suspicious circumstances. The manager met me at one of the rooms. She told me housekeeping found the sheets on one of the beds covered in blood. Another guest, who already checked out, told her he heard someone screaming in the room the night before. The guest said it wasn't a help-I'm-being-murdered scream. It was more of a hey-this-awesome-sex scream. He went on to say the screamer sounded like a man. I called Al at the police department on the phone and told him what I had. I asked him if he wanted me to secure the room and have an investigator come to the scene. He laughed. I asked, "What is so funny, Sarge?" He said, "You must think you are still in Mobile. We don't know what happened." I said, "Oh, believe me; I truly understand I am not in Mobile. I thought an investigator might want to come since there was so much blood, so maybe, oh I don't know, so someone could maybe investigate and maybe find out what happened. I forgot who I work for. For a minute I was thinking it was someone competent. Sorry to bother you."

I responded to domestic complaint at an apartment complex on Martin Luther King the next day. The boyfriend had moved out of the apartment about six weeks before. He returned to talk to his girlfriend, but she refused to speak to him. He broke the front window and climbed in. They got into an argument, which got really heated. He punched her several times, bruising her jaw and breaking her nose. I witnessed him punch her twice as I climbed through the window. After a brief struggle, I was able to cuff him. I transported him to the police department. Al was sitting in dispatch. He looked surprised when I walked in with a prisoner. He asked me what happened. He said or grunted, "That's a damn shame. I know his momma." I completed the paperwork and left.

Move Along; Nothing to See Here

At shift change I came back to the police department and realized my prisoner who was supposed to be going to the county jail in Brewton because he had two felony charges involving domestic violence was missing. I said, "Hey, Sarge, where is my prisoner?" He grunted, "I called his momma to come get him." Before I could say anything the oncoming shift supervisor said, "Where does he live? We will go get him." I told him and then I said, "Can I arrest Al for impersonating an officer?" No one answered my question. The oncoming shift had him back in the cell within fifteen minutes. I waited for them to come back, so I would no for sure he was locked up. I was transferred to a different shift the following week.

One night I was sent out to I65 to assist the state. Several thousand roofing nails had been dumped on the interstate between the Bay Minette exit and the Brewton exit. The state asked that I check on vehicles southbound that were disabled. I checked on several cars between the Atmore and Bay Minette exits; they had all called AAA or had someone on the way to help. The state received a 911 call north of the Atmore exit and sent me to check it out. I drove for about ten minutes when an Escambia deputy got on scene and found nothing in the area. I had passed a small white car stopped on the southbound side a few minutes earlier; I turned around in the medium. I found the vehicle and noticed a 70s model Ford truck was parked behind the car. It was on a dark stretch of the interstate and I didn't see them until I was on top of them. I stopped in front of the white car and walked back to them.

There were three young black females in the car; the driver told me they had called AAA. The driver of the truck walked up as I was talking to her. He said, "I will wait with them." Something about him didn't seem right; when he walked back to his truck, I asked the females if they were comfortable with him waiting with them. They said they were. They told me he stopped behind them and asked if they were okay; they told him they had called someone. He told them he would wait until help came. I left to answer a 911 call a few miles to the south on the interstate that turned out to be a prank call. They voice in the back of my head was screaming at me.

Darrell McMann

About twenty minutes later I turned north to head back to Atmore, when my dispatcher told me a state trooper wanted to meet me and gave me the mile marker where he was. When I got there the trooper walked up to me and asked me if I could describe the truck and the white male. I asked, "What happened?" About five minutes after I left, the male opened the driver's side door and tried to abduct the driver at knife point. My heart sank. He didn't realize there were three people in the car. One of them had a knife and went after him; he jumped in his truck and took off. I gave him a description of the truck and the male. I walked over to the girls and apologized. They said, "It isn't your fault. You asked if we were comfortable with him," I had always trusted the voice in the back of my head and promised myself to never ignore it again.

Two blocks behind the police department is an area known as the Blocks. There were two bottle clubs next to each other, the Chick A Dee and Happy Days, and between the two they usually attracted several hundred people on the weekends when the other local clubs closed. We could see both clubs from the back parking lot of the police department. A fight or two usually broke out whenever the clubs were open; we did what we could with four officers and several hundred people. The street would be packed with people hanging out and that make it impossible to drive through. We tried to get two officers in the parking lot before the crowd showed up, but most nights we were on calls and couldn't get there. We heard shots fired several times while trying to clear the area out and managed to break up a few small fights before they became all-out brawls. Some of the fights would end up at the police department when one of the participants decided they were outnumbered or outgunned.

Carl Prim and I were talking with a female in the lobby of the police department when the female she had been arguing with at the Chick A Dee came through the door and jumped her in front of us. While we were pulling them apart, two guys and another female came in. The two guys started fighting and the female who came in with them was eight months pregnant. She was screaming at everyone. The dispatcher called for help since it was happening in front of her.

Move Along; Nothing to See Here

I managed to grab female number two and drag her to the back. I threw her in a cell and ran back to the lobby. The two guys ended up back outside and left. Carl managed to get female number three outside; she was worked up pretty good. One of the guys who was fighting in the lobby came back a few minutes later. I asked him where the other guy was. He said, "That bitch is probably running back to Monroeville." He told us they were from Monroeville and had ridden together. I told him we were keeping female number two. He didn't seem to care.

Al was off duty one night and sitting at the bar of the Chick A Dee waiting on his chicken sandwich. He heard several gunshots outside, and then a guy fell through the front door. One of Atmore's more accomplished drug-induced idiots shot him in the backside. He came in the bar to finish him off but realized there were lots of witnesses and left. The guy that was shot drove himself to the hospital. Jesse Stallings and I responded to the hospital about twenty minutes later, when they called to report someone had shown up with a gunshot wound. As we were standing there, the drug-induced idiot walked through the emergency entrance into the ER and stood next to us. We looked at him and asked what was going on. He ignored us and stared at the victim. The victim was on his stomach and didn't see him when he walked in. He looked behind him and yelled, "Hey, that's the nigger that shot me!" Jesse and I grabbed him. We took him to the floor and cuffed him after a brief struggle. He admitted to shooting him and wanted to see if he was still alive.

Al came to the hospital a few minutes later. He still had some mayonnaise on his cheek from his chicken sandwich. He said, "I finished my chicken samich and figured I needed to come up here." I asked, "Were you in the Chick A Dee?" He said, "Yeah, I was gettin' a chicken samich, and I heard the shots. Then they came inside, and then they left. I decided I was going to eat my samich."

One night, actually very early in the morning, a white female came to the police department after everyone at the Blocks had left. She said a bunch of black girls threatened to beat and cut her if she came

Darrell McMann

back the next weekend. She said, "I don't want a report or anything, I just want some advice." I said, "Don't go back over there and that will solve your problem." She said, "Well, okay, I was hoping you would say something else."

The next weekend she showed up at the police department again after everyone had left the Blocks. She was breathing heavily and sweating profusely. Her clothes were torn, and she had a bloody nose. She told us one of the black girls that threatened her the previous weekend saw her and jumped on her. She said she ran away and hid until she felt it was safe to run back to her car. She said, "I don't want a report, but I need some advice." I said, "What did I tell you last week?" She said, "That I shouldn't go back." She said, "But I like black guys, and I think you are jealous." I laughed and said, "I could care less who you like, but you asked me what I thought, and I told you. You decided you didn't want to take my advice, and you went anyway. The girl kept her promise, you got whipped and then ran away and hid."

The next weekend she came back to the police department. She had a minor stab wound on her chest and said that several black females chased her down the street. I said, "Let me guess, you don't want a report, you just want some advice." She said, "I want her arrested." I said, "What does she look like?" She said, I don't know but several people saw it happen." "I said, "Where are they now?" She said, "I don't know." Then she said, "Well, I guess you were right, never mind." She got in her car and left.

A citizen called one Sunday night about two cars racing through the neighborhood ramming into each other. I was turning in the direction of the area where the caller last saw them. I noticed a truck heading east had stopped for the red light and appeared to have a lot of recent damage. Before I could turn, I saw a truck approaching the red light at a high rate of speed also from the east. The second truck rammed the first truck from behind, forcing it into the intersection. The force of the impact almost knocked the truck into me. The second truck lost control and ended up on the north side of the intersection

Move Along; Nothing to See Here

in the southbound lanes of highway 21. The church located on the corner had just ended their Sunday Night services.

I jumped out of my car and walked toward the second truck. The driver exited and started walking toward the first truck with an axe handle in his hand. I stepped in front of him with my gun drawn and ordered him to drop the weapon and go down to his knees. He did as I asked. He got down on his knees and then decided he wasn't going to jail. I was standing over him and noticed he was getting up so I put him in a headlock and forced him to the ground. I cuffed him after a brief struggle. Both guys were addicted to crystal methamphetamine. Idiot number one had shafted idiot number two over some dope. Idiot number two figured it out and decided to get even.

Kim started attending a Baptist church in Atmore on a regular basis. She asked me if I would come. It was the first Sunday for the new sanctuary. When I walked in, I saw the mayor shaking hands. I decided to make the best of it and avoided him. I looked at the choir and saw a businessman who was cavorting around town in his convertible Mustang with his seventeen-year-old girlfriend. I met him at his house one evening the week before because he wanted me to check out his house. He was afraid his wife was in the house hiding with a gun waiting to kill him. I noticed every light in the house was on; I asked him why all the lights were on. He told me he had been through the house and turned on every light as he went through each room to be sure no one was there. I asked him why he wanted me to go through the house. He said they were having problems; he wanted me to be a witness if it went to court. I asked, "A witness to what?" He said, "That I called the police, she threatened to kill me, and you searched the house." I told him I wasn't playing his stupid games. Before he could say anything else I left. He saw me sitting in the pew, and he waved and winked at me; I ignored him.

I was approached a couple of minutes later by the guy I had to fight in the middle of the street the week before after he wrecked his buddy over a bad drug deal. He presented his hand for me to shake, and I reluctantly shook hands. He apologized and told me it wouldn't happen again. I said, "Good." We fought about two weeks later when someone reported he was acting suspiciously. He was high again. He approached me the following Sunday and presented his hand for me to shake. I left him hanging and walked away.

I told Kim I didn't want to go back to church because of some of the people, and I explained why. I know I should have felt differently, but I couldn't sit with them on Sunday and then deal with them all week on the street.

In the summer of 1998 Kim was approached about taking the director's position at the hospital in Brewton; the administration wanted one director for the two departments. She felt like she could handle the additional responsibility. The department in Atmore was operating as she wanted, and she was confident in her assistant. We decided she should try. If it was too much, she would let the administrator know; they decided to try it for a few months to see if it would work. We decided to sell the trailer and move to Brewton. We fund a nice rental house in the country about three miles west of Brewton.

Kim got saved and was baptized before we moved to Brewton. I was saved in 1979 while sitting in class after lunch. My good friend, Bart Husby led me to the Lord back in middle school. I didn't really understand the significance of it until years later. I didn't change much of anything in my life, but I knew something was different. When Kim called her mother to tell her she was saved she said, "You don't know what you're doing."

Kim and I had been growing apart for some time. We decided to separate, so I moved out and rented an apartment in Atmore in January 1999. It was a mutual decision and we got along much better without the tension. Her mother called a few days after she found out we were separating. She told me she was going to miss me. I handed the phone to Kim.

Chapter 12

Sunday May 9, 1999 was a beautiful spring day; it was Mother's Day, and I had to work. Kim went to her parents that morning to drop off Elizabeth for a couple of days for a visit. She took some of their belongings to put in her parents' storage building. Kim was thinking about moving into an apartment.

It was an incredibly slow day. Around noon I walked into the police department, and the dispatcher asked if I knew Susan McMann. I said, "Yeah, that's Kim. Why?" He said, "I've got the county dispatcher on the line." He handed me the phone. I knew something bad was going on. The dispatcher told me she had been in an accident and was ejected from the vehicle. I knew then she was gone. I asked if she was okay. She said, "They have taken her to the hospital in Brewton." I knew she was taking Elizabeth to her parents but didn't know if she had come back so soon. I asked the dispatcher if a child was with her. She checked with the state trooper, and he advised that she was alone. I asked the dispatcher to call the chief and let him know I was going to Brewton. I gave him Kim's parents' home phone number and asked him to notify them.

I tried to convince myself she was okay even though I knew she wasn't. I walked in the hospital and told them who I was there for. I knew by the looks on their faces she was gone, but I continued to deny it to myself. It's hard to hide what you feel when you work with someone who has died, and you still have to do your job. I was told to wait just a minute and was led to a room. I was dreading the news that was coming. The door opened, and a doctor and a priest came in. I started breaking down. The doctor said, "I think you know what I'm going to tell you. I'm sorry." I became numb and almost got sick.

Kim's parents showed up with Elizabeth. She asked me why I was crying. I told her that her mommy was in heaven with God. She

Move Along; Nothing to See Here

seemed to understand. I didn't realize the hell I was about to go through with her family.

I was asked by someone at the hospital which funeral home I wanted to use. Kim's mother interrupted and said they had prepaid arrangements at a cemetery where they lived. News to me, but we had never really discussed where we wanted to be buried so I agreed.

Kim had hired an assistant director, Tina, shortly before I moved out. She was living in a motel room trying to find a place to live. When I moved, Kim told her she could move in until she found a place so she could save some money. It was also convenient because they were changing the way the department ran, and they were implementing new policies and procedures. They figured they could work on it at home instead of the hospital

I told Kim's parents and her sister that I was going to the house to tell Tina what happened and to get Kim's insurance policy. The dispatcher notified Chief Mac that Kim had been involved in a traffic accident, and I had left for Brewton. He drove to Brewton from his house to make sure I was okay. He told me he would drive me and get someone to come back and get my cruiser later. As we were leaving, I saw my dad walking up. We spoke for a few minutes, and he told me he would see me later at my apartment.

Kim's family showed up at the house about ten minutes before I did; the chief stayed in the car. I found her family in the house going through her paperwork; I didn't see Tina. I asked them what they were doing. Her dad said, "Helping you find the paperwork." I said, "I don't need your help I know exactly where it is." They quit looking. I asked them if they had seen Tina yet. Her mom said, "We told her, and she left." I thought that was a little strange. I found out later they drove up as Tina was mowing the yard. She walked over to them, and Kim's mother said, "Kim is dead and it's your fault." I found out the next day why she thought it was her fault.

Darrell McMann

Before we left the house I noticed Kim's parents and her sister walking through the house looking around. I was too upset to say anything and didn't know what they were doing. I realized later they were taking a quick inventory.

The next morning I packed enough clothing for four or five days and drove to their house. Before we left the house the night before, Kim's mom told me I could come stay at their house for the week since we needed to make all the arrangements. I thought that was a nice gesture. I didn't realize they were plotting. After I got there, we were sitting around the table when her dad said, "How do you feel about Tina taking your place?" I asked what he meant. He said, "Tina is a lesbian, and she turned Kim into one." I just sat there dumbfounded. Her mom said, "Yeah, Kim was queer when she died." I said, "What could have possibly given you that idea?" Her mom said, "She moved in as soon as you moved out." I tried to explain why Tina moved in, but they were convinced Kim had become a lesbian and told me I was in denial. I said, "If you knew Kim's beliefs you would know how she felt about it. Even if she was, why would you focus on that now? I think you need to remember things about her that made you happy." I was told I was in denial, so I said, "If she was, why dwell on it now? No one can do anything about it. She's gone." After three days of hearing it, I told them I suspected she was, hoping they would shut up.

The week I spent with them I was constantly asked if they were going to be a part of Elizabeth's life. Even though I couldn't stand to be around them, it was my desire for them to be a part of her life. They wouldn't let it rest and kept asking me. After I finally assured them that they would be a part of her life, I was informed it would be my responsibility to bring Elizabeth to them. It was too much of a hardship to meet me halfway. They kept on me about where Elizabeth and I were going to live. I told them I was intending on going back to Mobile. That wasn't good for them. I would have to get a job closer to them. I said, "I will think about it."

The day of the funeral, May 13, her mother told the funeral director she had some $100 certificates she wanted to use. She looked at

Move Along; Nothing to See Here

me and told me I could reimburse her later. I will never forget the look on the director's face.

I was surprised a few minutes later when Chief Mack walked in; he brought over half the police department with him in a show of support for me. I was speechless and everyone else thought it was a super nice thing to do. Kim's funeral escort was led by eight Atmore cruisers, the state trooper who investigated the crash, and two Escambia county cruisers.

The following day I called the attorney Kim had hired for our divorce. We decided to use one attorney since we were in agreement with everything. I wasn't sure if he knew she had died, and the divorce was supposed to be final the following week. He told me he had heard about it and told me how sorry he was. He filed paperwork to stop the process. He told me he was surprised that we had actually decided to get a divorce because we got along so well. I thanked him and was about to hang up, when he said, "I need to tell you something that's just unbelievable." I didn't say anything. He said, "Kim's family contacted me. They wanted me to find a loophole to make the divorce go through. I told them I couldn't do that. They wanted to get access to Kim's life insurance policy and the monthly social security payment Elizabeth would be receiving every month." I wasn't surprised. I called them later that day, so we could work out a time to meet at the house in Brewton. They had a large storage building on their property. I thought they might feel better knowing I wanted to store Kim's belongings on their property. We agreed to meet at 8:00 A.M. on Saturday May 15. I talked to Tina and told her we were coming to get Kim's things. She decided she didn't want to be there.

I got to the house ten minutes early, and found Kim's brother trying to pick the lock. We had a brief discussion about him committing burglary. We went in, and they started going through every drawer and started taking whatever they could grab. I told them to stop and put whatever they had back where it was. I showed them exactly what I wanted them to take to keep for me which was a large portion of what was in the house. They seemed to go along with it.

Darrell McMann

Just before we left I was informed that I was going to have to prove to them I was going to do the right thing. They didn't define what the right thing was but I was sure it was whatever they thought the right thing was. They questioned why I didn't bring Elizabeth. I told them she was at my parents. I was meeting my parents the next day to get the rest of our things and store them in one of their sheds. I told them I was planning on bringing Elizabeth to them tomorrow afternoon. I was going to be busy the first part of the following week with hiring an attorney to handle Kim's estate and go through all her paperwork for bills and other paperwork. I also told them I didn't think it was a good idea for her to be here while we were moving things out of the house. After all, her mother just died. They then had the gall to question who would have access to my parents' shed and wanted to know if I planned on using anything. Before we left, Kim's brother walked through the house with a video camera and recorded everything that was left in the house.

The next day I met my parents and then I took Elizabeth to them to stay for two or three days. Kim's parents were waiting for me on their front porch. They told me that the reason Kim and I were divorcing was because all of Kim's friends convinced her I was cheating on her. They accused me of sleeping with Tina or a girl that works at the cleaners in Atmore. They repeated their accusation that Tina is a lesbian and had turned Kim into one. They reproached me for not kicking Tina out of the house when she took my place. They wanted partial custody of Elizabeth. They stated that if we lived with my parents, Elizabeth wouldn't be safe. They told me I wasn't doing the right thing and that if I ever got married again, my new wife would hate Elizabeth because stepparents hate their stepchildren.

I spoke with Kim's oldest friend, Beth Sanders, during the week I spent at Kim's parents' house. Kim told me that when she was in high school, her mother threw all her things in the yard and forced her out of the house at gunpoint. She left and lived with Beth and her parents. Beth told me whatever that I do, don't give them any legal control over Elizabeth. Kim told her after Elizabeth was born she didn't want her mother to have any influence in Elizabeth's life. I told Beth the things Kim's parents were saying. She told me Kim knew I wasn't cheating on her, and she laughed at the lesbian accusation.

I spoke with several of her other friends over next couple of days. Melissa Hunt told me Kim had spoken to her about her parents influence over Elizabeth if anything ever happened to her. I told her what they said. She told me they were full of crap and wanted to go get them. Ann Bonds, who worked with Kim at the hospital in Atmore, and her husband had become close friends of both Kim and I. Ann told me that Kim told her recently she knew she was a good friend, and a good mother, but not much of a wife. I didn't agree with that. Ann told me not to believe anything her family said.

Having spoken with several of Kim's very good friends since the funeral, I didn't think much of her family's barrage of bull they threw at me on the porch. I was curious about the girl at the cleaners. I was told they had sources. I kind of laughed and let it go. They told me they wanted partial custody of Elizabeth because they were afraid I wouldn't be a good parent. I laughed at that too. They were concerned about Elizabeth being at my parents' house because my brother was living with them, and he had been arrested a couple times recently for being an idiot. He had already told me that he would move out if Elizabeth and I decided to come back to Mobile. I didn't tell them because I didn't think it would change how they felt. I asked them to define what they meant by "doing the right thing." Kim's mom said, "You know what we mean."

I told them I didn't want to talk about Tina anymore. I said, "You can't decide if she was a lesbian, heterosexual, or bisexual. You accused me of sleeping with her and Kim of sleeping with her. I'm surprised you haven't claimed we had a threesome. I didn't like her. I couldn't kick her out of the house; I didn't live there. Kim and I were legally separated. If Tina refused to allow me in the house, I would have to get a court order. I put aside my personal feelings to do what needed to be done. If something was going on between the two of them, I'm sure Elizabeth would have seen something and started asking questions." They didn't anticipate that and couldn't say anything.

Darrell McMann

When I left, I wanted to take Elizabeth with me and never come back. At the same time, I thought if I left her with them for a few days it would show them I was trying to keep them in Elizabeth's life.

Ann and Bob invited me over for dinner the next night. They knew my hours were crazy, and I wanted to go back to Mobile or go to work in Pensacola. They lived on five acres in the country about halfway between Atmore and Pensacola. They asked if I would think about moving in with them. They had a spare bedroom that Elizabeth could use. There was a small apartment or mother-in-law suite on the property that I could live in and pay them rent. Elizabeth would be able to stay with me the nights I was off. I thought it was a great idea and decided to do it.

On May 19, I drove back to Kim's parents' to get Elizabeth; I met Kim's sister in a parking lot. Just before she pulled away she said, "You ain't doing things right." She drove away before I could respond. Elizabeth and I went to my parents for the weekend to relax.

I called Kim's mom on May 21 and told her Elizabeth and I would be moving to Bob and Ann's; I explained the arrangements. She didn't like it, and I thought she was about to hyperventilate. She got herself together and hung up.

On Saturday morning May 22, I was sitting in my parents' living room watching a movie. It was the first time I had been able to relax since Kim died. Then Kim's mom called. She said, "I have been watching the tape, and I saw some things I want." I told her I was going to the house Monday morning to get our things from the shed and bring them to their house to store them there. Whatever is left in the house is Tina's property. They had some clothing of Elizabeth's that was there that I wanted to get. She didn't agree with any of it. I said, "I've had enough. You haven't listened to a damn thing I've said from the beginning. You think you can do or say anything you please. Now you're sitting around watching your own home version of the Home Shopping Network. I'll see ya Monday morning at your house." She hung up before I could.

Move Along; Nothing to See Here

Kim's sister called me about an hour later. She told me I'm not doing things right and informed me that Kim was rebellious and just wanted to go to the beach. I said, "Listen up! How can you say she was rebellious? She was a straight-A student, never got in trouble, put herself through school, and loaned ya'll money whenever you needed it." We had taken out a $5,000 loan a few months before Kim died, so her sister could purchase a used van. I said, "You're late on the loan payment." She hung up. I never got another penny from her and paid it off myself.

I was so pissed I called Bob and asked him if he was busy the next day, Sunday. He said he was going on a ride with some friends and asked me what was up. I told him what was going on and that I wanted to get the stuff to them a day earlier. He said, "Yeah, I'll help you. We can just ride to Brewton and then on to their house. They may not like five Harleys coming down their driveway, but who cares? We may take care of them ourselves." We laughed.

That Sunday morning we headed to Brewton—me in my Ranger, pulling a utility trailer and five Harleys. We loaded up the trailer and headed to their house. We showed up at their house, but no one was home; we decide to go to the Golden Corral for lunch. I was so worked up I couldn't eat, so I told Bob's friends everything that had happened. One of them said, "I think I'll stay here I'm liable to hurt somebody." We drove back to their house after lunch; they were home.

We unloaded the trailer, and as soon as we finished, Kim's sister tried to start an argument with me. I ignored her. Her mother told her to leave, and as she drove away, she extended her middle finger indicating how high her IQ was. I yelled, "Is that your IQ?" She stopped, but her mother yelled at her to leave. Kim's mother asked me if they are going to able to see Elizabeth again." I asked, "Have I done or said anything that would give you reason to think I wouldn't allow you to see her?" She shook her head no. I asked for Elizabeth's clothes. She said, "You can't come in the house." I said, "Okay, I will wait right here." Her mother said, "Kim wanted me to sort them." I said, "I can sort them." Kim's dad said, "You are going to have to bring the sheriff."

Darrell McMann

I said, "Are you sure?" He turned and walked away. I said, "Okay." I drove back to Grand Bay.

Kim's mom called me two days later and asked if I was calm enough to talk. I said, "Nope" and hung up. She called me back a few minutes later. I decided she could talk to the answering machine. She said she wanted Elizabeth to have her things. I go about me business. I returned her call the following the day. No one was home, so I left a message. I asked them to put her things in garbage bags, set them out by the gate, and I would come pick them up. They didn't like that idea. We traded a few messages throughout the day.

Kim's mother called the next day and left a message. She said, "Everything will be ready for you. You can come get it, and you won't have to speak to anyone." I liked that idea, so I called her back and left a message that I would be there around 9:00 A.M. Saturday morning.

I recruited Carl Prim to go with me. We showed up at 9:20 A.M., and I immediately noticed there are no bags, and there is a lock and chain on the gate. I said, "They have never locked the gate before. I wonder why it's locked?" I decided right then I wasn't playing anymore of their stupid games. They could keep her clothes, and I would just buy her new clothes. As I was about to get in my truck and leave, I noticed Kim's dad walking toward me; I waited to see what he had to say.

He said, "Can we talk like men?" I said, "I have tried, but I'm tired of playing stupid games." I reminded him that they agreed to the plan that we worked out for this morning. I said, "I didn't come here to talk to anyone. I've tried, and nobody has listened to anything I have said." He said, "We didn't know you were coming this morning. Can we talk?" I said, "No, I have had enough." As I'm getting in my truck he said, "Go to hell!" I said, "Okay." Carl and I drove back to Atmore.

Kim's mother called me on June 1, and said that she wanted Elizabeth to have some of her clothes. I asked, "Why not all of them?" She said, "She can have more the next time we see her." I laughed and said, "I'll think about it." I hung up.

Move Along; Nothing to See Here

During the message trading, I had gone to the hospital in Atmore to speak with Kim's supervisor, Paula Jones, and to sign forms related to her benefits. Paula and Kim had become good friends; Paula was responsible for leading Kim to the Lord. She told me that Kim had hoped that we would eventually get back together and that she felt like it was her fault our marriage didn't work. I said, "Whatever happened was my fault, too." She also told me she was happy about our living arrangements. Kim had shared many stories about her mother with Paula. I talked to her about what was going on with Kim's family since she had died. Paula asked me if I wanted to write them a letter to get everything off my chest, and she offered to help me. She said it would be therapeutic. She told me she was upset about the pastor her mother picked for the services. She said, "He didn't even know her." I said, "It's a pattern because her family didn't know her either." I sent them the letter on June 2.

Four days later, Kim's sister called and left a message on my answering machine. Apparently I am less than a man. The first chance she gets she is going to tell Elizabeth about her daddy. I didn't do things right after Kim died, and Kim was a liar. She couldn't understand why I couldn't work with them. I played it a couple of times, and I couldn't believe how stupid this was. On June 14, Kim's brother showed up at the police department in Atmore and asked the dispatcher to call me at home. I told the dispatcher to tell him I would be there in a thirty minutes. He was the most reasonable one of the bunch, so I thought maybe we could work something out.

I was wrong. He told me Kim had exaggerated things, and she had gotten married because she was lonely. He wanted to put everything from the house in a rental storage unit. I reminded him that Kim and I had accumulated the furniture and all the other stuff while we were married. Renting a storage unit would be stupid. He asked if I was going to get a court order. He was afraid his mother would destroy everything in the shed if she thought I was going end up getting it. He told me he would speak to them and get back to me. He never did.

Darrell McMann

I thought about going to court but decided against it. They could keep it for Elizabeth when she got older. They could explain to her why they kept things that belonged to her and her mother. I was tired of dealing with them.

Six weeks after Kim passed away, I had an interview with the Pensacola Police Department. I was still in a haze from Kim's death, and I don't remember anything about the interview. I looked out the window toward the end when I got tears in my eyes. I'm not sure if they noticed. I passed the interview, so they set me up with a physical. During the examination, the doctor found that I had an inguinal hernia. He was down there for so long, I almost asked him to marry me.

Sergeant Black, who was the training/personnel supervisor, told me if I had the surgery and it went well, the department would hire me and place me on light duty. I scheduled the surgery later that afternoon. He called me a couple weeks later—I would start on September 20, 1999.

Chapter 13

The city of Pensacola has a population of about 55,000 people. The police department at the time had 162 officers; I had never worked around K9 units before, so that was going to be a new experience.

My first FTO was Kelly White, and I was her first trainee. She told me later she was nervous because I had more experience, and I had been an FTO. She was knowledgeable and a very good officer. She helped me get acclimated to my new surroundings.

We were running radar one evening in the parking lot of Miles Furniture on Bayou Boulevard when a vehicle sped past us heading east toward Ninth Avenue. I took off after it. She said, "There is a hump up here." I looked at her and nodded. I was picking up speed as we closed in on the vehicle. She said, "There is a hump up here." I nodded again and thought, "Geeze, I heard you the first time." As we entered the intersection she yelled, "THERE IS A HUMP HERE!" I couldn't respond. We hit the hump. The car went airborne, and we were in the ceiling. We were laughing so hard I almost couldn't stop the car. It took me a few minutes to regain my composure before I could approach the vehicle.

We responded to a suicide on the north end of town close to Halloween. When we arrived, we met two teenagers in the driveway who were extremely upset. One of them said, "She's in the garage." The kids practically grabbed Kelly, so I checked out the garage. I found a female, their mother, hanging from a rope. I had never worked a suicide by hanging, and I thought for a second that someone was trying to pull a Halloween prank until I got a close look. She had been there for a while; apparently your neck can stretch pretty far.

My second FTO was Tom Glaud. Tom had been a FTO for a while and tried to get me worked up to see how I would react. I knew what he was doing and didn't let it bother me until one night just before the end of the shift. Someone called 911 from a neighborhood in the

Move Along; Nothing to See Here

central part of the city. We were on the extreme southwest edge of town. No other unit in the city volunteered to take it, so Tom said, "Let's go!" I looked at the map book real quick and took off. The witness told dispatch a couple minutes later that the suspect was walking down the street; two or three units advised they were in the area.

I found the street. I saw a couple units at the end of the street and was heading to them. Tom said, "Aren't you going to look at any house numbers?" I pointed down the street and said, "There are several units at the end of the street." He said, "I don't care what they are doing—look for an address!" Needless to say, he kinda ticked me off. I slammed on the brakes and yanked the spotlight to the left. I happened to stop directly in front of the house. I couldn't have planned it any better. I said, "It's right here!" We got out and found the sliding-glass door had been broken out. I thought it was funny that I just happened to stop in front of the house without having any idea which part of the block I was in.

Since I had prior experience, I skipped the third phase with Kelly and went to my two-week fourth phase. Ed Grim was my FTO. Ed is a unique person. There is only one of him, thank the Lord.

December 31, 1999, the world was filled anxiety from the uncertainty surrounding what would happen at the stroke of midnight. The department adjusted schedules and brought in over 100 officers for the big event.

Pensacola, like Atmore, has an area known as the Blocks. There is a bottle club at Belmont and Devilliers along with a chicken stand. I was thinking they would keep a majority of the officers on duty until at least 5:00 A.M., when the Blocks crowd headed home. By 3:00 A.M., every extra officer had been sent home.

Another officer and I were on Belmont Street about two or three blocks from the bottle club when we heard several shots fired. We couldn't get very far in our cruisers because of the crowd; we began walking toward the bottle club. A guy ran up to me and said he had

Darrell McMann

been stabbed, and I could see that he had a serious stab wound on his side below his rib cage. I looked back and saw another officer pulling up. I told him to go to that officer, and he would call an ambulance. We got about a half-block from the bottle club when we came upon three separate fights; we heard a few more gunshots down the street. I took my pepper spray and sprayed everyone who was fighting. It had the desired affect—they all stopped fighting, started coughing, and ran away.

We got to the end of the block, and a female ran up to us and pointed south to the next intersection. She pointed at a guy and said, "That nigger has a gun!" He wasn't facing us, so he didn't see us running toward him; he turned around when we got within twenty feet of him. My partner was directly in front of him and ordered him at gunpoint to show us his hands. The guy looked confused, he kept his hands in his coat pockets. He ordered him to show his hands again, but he just kept looking at him like he was confused. I approached him from the side and pepper sprayed him. I patted him down real quick, but he didn't have a gun. Someone else ran up to us and said the guy with the gun had left in a car.

The final tally for the evening: one person was stabbed, about a dozen people were pepper sprayed, lots of lead was flying around, and several hundred people were running around like a stampeding herd of cattle.

I was transferred to the day shift a couple weeks later. One of my first calls came as we were finishing lineup; it was a domestic complaint that involved a male who refused to leave a house. Paris Hilton, who was working midnights, got on the radio and advised me that she had been there three times since midnight, and she would handle it. I thought to myself, "I am not going three times, so I will go anyway."

As I drove up to the scene, I observed Paris standing in the middle of the intersection with a black male. I exited my cruiser and walked up to them. Paris said, "I am going to tell you in front of this officer that I am tired of coming here. You are wasting MY time." She grabbed

Move Along; Nothing to See Here

her badge and said, "Do you see this? Do you know who I am?" The guy looked at me, and I looked at him. We both wanted to know who she was. Actually I wanted to say to him, "I don't know who she is, but I will grab her, so you can smack her around for a few minutes." He tried to say something, but she told him to shut up because she was tired of listening to him. He was still a little drunk and was obviously tired. I said, "Hey man, which house is yours?' He pointed. I said, "If I can get you a change of clothes, do you have somewhere you can go for a while until you and your wife calm down?" He said, "Yes, that's what I have been trying to do for the last four hours, but no one will listen to me." I got him a change of clothes. He looked at me and said, "Thank you, officer. Thanks for listening." He gave Paris a dirty look. I told him he was welcome.

One afternoon I was dispatched to a residence for a "drunk refusing to leave call." When I arrived, the caller contacted me as I was exiting my cruiser. She pointed at a black male sitting on a bicycle in the street and said, "That's him but I think everything is good now." She walked back to her apartment. I walked over to the bicyclist and asked what was going on. He said, "I'm drunk. I am at the wrong apartment. I thought someone I know lived here. She told me they didn't live here, and I got mad and started talking crazy. I told her I was sorry." I told him I appreciated his honesty. While we were speaking, my backup, Wanda Sykes, showed up. She spoke with the complainant briefly and then approached the confused intoxicated bicyclist.

Wanda said, "What the hell is your problem you drunk son of a bitch?" He got off of his bicycle, and they started arguing. I grabbed him by the arm and walked him two houses over. He said, "She ain't going to talk to me like that. I don't care if she is an officer or not." I told him not to worry about Wanda, just talk to me. He calmed down a little. My warrant check came back negative, so I told him he could go.

Wanda wandered back over and said something ugly to him. Next thing I know they are fighting on the ground at my feet. He punched her couple of times before I could cuff him. I should have let Wanda

Darrell McMann

handle the arrest, but I was so aggravated with her I decided I would take care of it.

A couple of weeks later a state attorney called me. He wanted to know the circumstances leading up to the arrest. I told him to call Wanda. He did, and I didn't get another call or a subpoena for court.

One afternoon I responded to an assault complaint in the Sanders Beach neighborhood. I knocked on the door. The home owner opened the door and extended his hand. He introduced himself as Doctor Jones. He looked at me as if he smelled something terrible. I wanted to say, "Hi, I'm Officer McMann, and I don't care if you're a big shot doctor." I smiled and asked him how I could help him. He smiled, too, but still looked at me with his nose pointed straight in the air.

He told me he wanted his neighbor arrested for assault. I asked him what happened. Dr. Big Shot was a high-ranking honcho in the Sanders Beach Neighborhood Association. He and several other neighbors were displeased with the appearance of his neighbor's property. The doctor saw his neighbor raking leaves and decided to discuss the issue with him; the doctor said it got pretty heated. He said he realized he wasn't getting anywhere and walked away. He quit talking, and I said, "So when did the assault take place?" The doctor said, "He was armed with a rake." I said, "Did he threaten you with it or make any overt movements that would make you believe he was going to strike you?" He said, "No." I said, "It isn't an assault." He looked at me like I was completely clueless and said, "He was armed with a rake!" I said, "He was raking leaves when you confronted him. You told me he didn't threaten you with the rake, and you didn't feel like he was going to hit you with it. You even turned your back on him and walked away." He said, "What would your sergeant say?" I said, "He would say, 'What did Officer McMann tell you?' After you told him what I said, he would say that he agreed with my decision."

I walked to my cruiser and got my statute book. I read him the definition of assault. He said, "What about battery?" I said, "For it to be

Move Along; Nothing to See Here

a battery he would have to strike you." He said, "Thanks for nothing and went in his house."

Kim's sister called the dispatcher while I was on duty in late March of 2000. She told the dispatcher I didn't know her but she had an urgent message for me. I decided to call her to see what she had to say. She wanted to get together and talk. I told her I would meet her when I got off work at the end of the week at the Burger King on Davis Highway near the mall.

When we met she told me that Kim had a private investigator follow me. I said, "He must have been really bored because I pretty much went to work and then home." She said Kim made me spend time with Elizabeth. I laughed at that. She said that she and her parents were afraid someone would take over my decision making. I laughed. She said they didn't understand why I was so angry. I laughed again. She said someone overheard my parents tell me to get Elizabeth away from her family. I asked who overheard it, but she wasn't sure. She said that I had given Elizabeth to Ann. I said, "I have a receipt." She didn't think that was funny. She said, "MY MOM LIKES YOU." I almost fell out of my chair. Then she said that she was afraid my brother would break into my parents shed and take my stuff, I got up and left.

I responded several times to complaints about prostitutes in the Brownsville area. One girl in particular was giving some of the residents a lot of grief. If she thought someone was complaining about her she would pace back and forth on the street in front of the person's house. She would curse loudly if children were around and would wave down prospective clients. After about five complaints in two days, I was as frustrated as the people who lived there. I tried to catch her flagging cars and getting into a vehicle, but I was never in the right place at the right time. She was a real joy to speak to—to say our personalities didn't jibe was an understatement.

I responded to the fifth complaint and saw her walking. It was in the middle of the day in mid-July; the temperature was in the mid 90s and the humidity was about 150 percent. What I'm saying is; it was hot. I pulled up next to her and cracked my window. She said, "I ain't doing nothing, so just keep going." I rolled my window down and said, "Man, it's hot out there. I'm glad my AC works. You look like you just got out of a hot shower. I bet you would like a nice cold bottle of water." I took a long sip of water and slowly rolled my window up. She wasn't happy. I drove next to her for a few minutes until she walked into the county. I remembered during one of our wonderful conversations she told me her ex-boyfriend had infected her with HIV. The department had just installed laptops in our cruisers, and we had access to our records and the county's records. I parked under a nice shade tree to conduct some research.

I noticed she made a complaint with the sheriff's office in 1997; I pulled up the report. She reported her boyfriend told her he had contracted HIV, and she had been infected. I didn't see any arrest reports or any other offense reports. I read the statute for criminal transmission of HIV or other STDs. I formed several questions to ask her.

The next morning I saw her walking down the same street; I stopped and called her over to me. She said, "What is it now?" I said, "I just need to ask you a few things." I whipped out my Miranda card and read her rights to her. She said, "What are you doing that for?" I said, "I'm going to ask you a few questions." She said, "Okay." She became a little defensive when I started asking questions about her past, but she answered the questions for me. When I finished I said, "Okay, thank you." She shrugged her shoulders and walked into the county.

I typed up an arrest affidavit and sent it to a judge. The judge found there was probable cause and signed it. I served the warrant on her a couple days later. She wasn't happy. On the way to the jail, I asked if she knew for sure that she had HIV. She said, "My boyfriend told me he had it, so I figured I gotta have it." I asked, "You have never been tested, but you just assumed you have it?" She said, "Yep." I told her she needed to be tested. I'm not sure if she ever did or not. I only saw her once briefly after I arrested her. One of the other girls told me a couple weeks later she went back to the East Coast to live with her family.

Move Along; Nothing to See Here

Kim's sister called again in October of 2000; she said she couldn't remember anything we had talked about previously. She asked me why did I hate them and why couldn't we resolve things? She said that she couldn't understand why I couldn't let things go. I said, "What things are you talking about? I thought you didn't remember anything." She got mad. I asked about our furniture, but she didn't want to discuss it. I reminded her of the loan that I was paying that I took out for her. She didn't know what I was talking about. I said, "Don't call me again. This isn't fun anymore." I hung up.

I met my future wife, Cindy White, in November of 2000. We met through her best friend Samantha; she is a criminal analyst in investigations at the police department. We hit it off right away, and Elizabeth took to her quickly, too. Cindy and I decided we were getting married within a couple months. I liked her parents as soon as I met them, and they actually made me feel welcome.

Cindy is eight years younger than me and didn't have any children. She was and still is a member of Pensacola Baptist Temple; Elizabeth and I started attending the church regularly. I had never been around such friendly people. The pastor, Gary Sanderson, was and still is an awesome man of God. He tells you how it is and doesn't tickle your ears. I got my heart and head right with God, and Elizabeth would eventually accept the Lord as her savior.

I purchased a vacant lot in Cantonment just north of Pensacola in the summer of 2000. I contracted with a builder and moved into the house in March of 2001. I felt like I had finally gotten to where I wanted to be in life.

While the house was under construction, the neighbor whose property adjoined mine made a pest of himself to the foreman building my house. The neighborhood is on an incline and his property is at the end of the hill. His property is basically shaped like a bowl, and he wasn't happy when my lot was cleared.

Darrell McMann

A few weeks before the house was finished, it was raining cats and dogs; red dirt was being washed into his backyard. He called the foreman at home on a Saturday night complaining. The foreman told him he couldn't do anything now because it was raining. My neighbor said, "That's okay. The red dirt is forming a barrier and keeping the rainwater runoff away from my house." He hung up.

Elizabeth and I came home after I picked her up from daycare the first Monday I was in the house. I was taking my uniform off when I heard the doorbell ring; I answered the door, and it was my neighbor. He said, "You need to come with me and look at this." I said, "What?" He said, "Where the rain has been going." I said, "I'm busy. I'm having some dirt delivered tomorrow, and a friend is going to spread it for me tomorrow afternoon. I have grass coming Wednesday, and I have taken Thursday and Friday off to lay sod. That should take care of your problem." He started to complain, but I said, "I'm busy, and we have to be somewhere in about fifteen minutes. He stomped off.

I came home the next day and found a notice of violation taped to my front door from county code enforcement for not having grass. Needless to say, I was a little aggravated.

I had the dirt delivered and spread. The grass was delivered Thursday around noon; I had several friends coming over on Friday for a sod-laying party. I decided I would lay a few rows Thursday afternoon. I had been throwing sod for about an hour when I noticed a county code enforcement truck parked down the street. The code enforcement officer finally got out of his truck and approached me. He looked at my cruiser and said, "I didn't know you were an officer." I shrugged my shoulders. He said, "Your neighbor told me that you told him you were going to be laying sod today." I said, "It's amazing when someone does what they say they are going to do." He got back in his truck and left.

Apparently that didn't satisfy my neighbor. He called code enforcement after I had more work done to raise the level of the

Move Along; Nothing to See Here

easement separating our properties. An officer left a note on my door stating they were having a meeting at my house with the builder and noted the date and time. He wrote "You may attend the meeting." I thought, "That's nice of them to invite me to a meeting at my house."

The builder was invited to attend also. We all met at the appointed time. The county engineer was talking to my builder while we waited for my neighbor to join us. As soon as he walked out of his back door, he started bad-mouthing my builder. I thought the builder was going to jump the fence and whip my neighbor. I was going to help him over the fence if he needed my help. The county engineer looked at me, but realized I was enjoying the argument, so he decided to be the peacemaker. My neighbor's issue was the French drain that ran the length of the easement. He told my builder that he'd watched two of his guys dig it up and then put a plug in the end of it. My builder asked, "Did you tell my foreman what you saw?" He said, "I haven't told anyone until right now." I thought my builder was going to explode. He told the county engineer he would have a couple of guys come by the next day and repair the drain. Everyone was happy.

September 11, 2001 was a beautiful day. One of those days you wonder why you are at work. I was working on a burglary report when Sharon Barber sent me an e-mail about a plane hitting the World Trade Center. I thought it was a Cessna and asked her if she was ready for some coffee. I walked into the Good Neighbor coffee shop on Garden Street to get some coffee, and the TV was on. As I placed my order, the second plane hit Tower Two. I knew then that life had just changed, and someone just declared war on us. I stood there for several minutes in disbelief as did everyone all over the world.

I didn't do anything the rest of the day unless I was dispatched to a call. I was listening to the news when it was announced that a plane hit the Pentagon and another plane went down in Pennsylvania. I wondered if there were more and wanted to do something. I spent my off days glued to CNN. When we attacked the Taliban in Afghanistan I felt like our country was on the right track. Our country has gone off track since.

I had to go to the Naval Hospital to contact one of the drivers of a traffic crash I was investigating a couple of weeks after 9/11. Large concrete barricades had been placed at the entrance to the hospital for security reasons. I pulled up next to a private who was posted at the entrance to the hospital. He looked at me for a minute. I knew by the look on his face he didn't know what to do with me. I was in a marked cruiser and in uniform. I said, "Would you like to see my ID?" He said, "Yeah." He held it for about thirty seconds. I said, "You don't know what to do with me, do you?" He said, "No, I sure don't." I said, "You want me to go see the sergeant? I noticed a sergeant was posted about fifty yards away. He said, "Yeah, go see him," and he gave me my ID back.

I pulled up next to the sergeant who gave me the same look. I handed him my ID. He looked at it for a while. I said, "You don't know what to do with me, do you?" He said, "No I don't. Why are you here?" I told him what I was doing, and he called a lieutenant. He asked the lieutenant, "Should I take his weapon?" The lieutenant said, "Don't bother. If he was a terrorist, he would have already shot you." The sergeant said, "I guess you can go."

Cindy and I were married on November 10, 2001, two weeks after Samantha married Mark Mims. They started dating a few weeks before Cindy and I met. We were in each other's weddings.

The pastor and I were waiting to walk out during the ceremony; he looked through the glass in the door and said, "This is the biggest wedding I have ever done. I'm kind of nervous." I said, "You think you're nervous. How do you think I feel?" The ceremony was great, and Cindy was a beautiful bride.

Cindy asked me shortly after we were married if I minded if she adopted Elizabeth. I didn't mind—I thought it was a great idea.

During lineup one morning the lieutenant mentioned something about having problems with his daughter. He was extremely frustrated with her. It got quiet for a couple seconds when Jim Carey said, "Yeah,

Move Along; Nothing to See Here

Lieutenant, I was listening on my scanner. I don't blame you for being pissed." We couldn't believe he just said that. A couple of us decided at the end every phone conversation to say, "Oh, by the way, Carey sucks." We saw Carey at the end of the day, when we turned in our paperwork, and he seemed like he was mad about something. I said, "Hey, Jim what's wrong? You look upset." He gave me a dirty look and left.

I responded to the intersection of E and Government in reference to a single vehicle traffic crash. I contacted the driver, who was being treated by EMTs in the back of the ambulance. He asked me if I saw a guy wearing shorts in the vacant lot across the street from where his car came to a sliding stop. I asked, "Are talking about the white guy with no shirt, blue jean shorts with the oh-no-it's-the-police look on his face?" He said, "Yeah, that's probably him."

The driver told me he was heading west on Government Street when one of his front tires exploded. He slammed on his brakes about fifty feet east of the intersection, which caused his vehicle to lose control. When the right front tire hit the curb on the northwest side of the intersection the vehicle flipped onto its left side and slid another seventy-five feet west on Government Street. The vehicle came to a rest on all four tires when it stopped sliding. The driver noticed the Good Samaritan run over to him from the vacant lot across the street. The Good Samaritan opened the driver side door and told the driver to remain calm and that he was going to help him out of the vehicle. He helped him out of the vehicle and sat him down in the street. He told the driver he was going to get a towel he had seen in his vehicle. The driver noticed he was taking a long time looking for the towel when another bystander approached him.

The bystander, soon to be witness, was stopped at the intersection and had watched the crash as it occurred. He also watched the Good Samaritan remove him from the vehicle and then go back to the vehicle. He noticed the driver looked like he was okay, so he had walked over to see what the Good Samaritan was doing. The Good Samaritan was stuffing his pockets with all the change from the console—almost $50 in change. The witness said, "HEY WHAT ARE YOU DOING? GET OUT OF THERE! The Good Samaritan then walked back over to the vacant lot.

The witness approached me as I was exiting the ambulance. He asked me if the driver told me what happened. I told him he did but I needed to get a statement from him after I talked to the Good Samaritan. He told me he would wait by his truck.

I took a quick look at the vehicle and then I found the Good Samaritan sipping a Bud Light under a nice shade tree in the vacant lot. Before I could say anything he said, "I was going to use some of his change to walk over to Shoreline, a block and half away, to get him a bottle of water." I asked, "Didn't you see the bottle of water in the cup holder that is about three-quarters full?" Instead of answering he said, "I got in his car to get the towel to wipe the sweat from his face. When I saw all that change I figured someone should make sure no one steals it." I said, "What towel? I didn't see a towel." He said, "It must have been a shirt." I said, "Turn around you're under arrest."

I notified dispatch that I had made an arrest for an incident unrelated to the crash. Robert Leeks, who was working a neighboring beat, advised me he would take the traffic crash for me. A few minutes later a recently promoted sergeant showed up. The sergeant asked me what happened. When I finished with the story, the sergeant asked, "We can make an arrest?" I didn't answer for a few seconds because I wasn't sure if they were serious. I said, "Yes it's not only a petty theft it's a…" The sergeant interrupted me and said, "I will go ask Officer Leeks." The sergeant walked back over to me and said, "Officer Leeks said it's a burglary." I said, "Yeah, it's a vehicle burglary and a petty theft." The sergeant said, "Well, how about that," and left.

Chapter 14

In the spring of 2002, I transferred from patrol to work the mall detail. Three mall officers are assigned to the traffic division and work all parades and other special events in the city. We worked ten-hour shifts and had weekends off every other month; we were off on Sundays. I worked with Bart Yolanski, aka Ski, and Jeff Henderson. Very few people know it but Ski does an awesome impression of the Cowardly Lion from the movie *The Wizard of Oz*. He even looks like the lion when he does it.

Ski was the officer in charge at the mall and handled our work schedules. One of us came in at 10:00 A.M. and got off at 8:00 P.M. The other officer worked from 12:00 noon to 10:00 P.M. We usually had two officers on duty every day. The mall provided us with a radio in case the security guards needed our assistance. As mall security, Parisian Loss Prevention had access to the same frequency and could also contact us.

My first day at the mall, Ski had to go to training, so I was working alone. One of the loss prevention officers from Parisian called me on the radio. He told me they had been watching a black male for several minutes. They observed him walk out to his car several times and felt like he was about to leave the store. I met them in the parking lot next to the suspect's car; the back seat was filled with clothing that had obviously been stolen. The loss prevention officer told me they might not be able to arrest them because of their store policy. They can't make an arrest if they lose sight of the suspect. He told me was going to call his boss. I told him to do that, and I would back off and watch the vehicle.

I drove across the parking lot to watch it from a distance when dispatch called me. One of the department's narcotics officers wanted me to call him. I called him, and he asked me if I was watching a blue Buick Regal in front of Parisian; I told him I was. He said, "The car

Move Along; Nothing to See Here

belongs to a CI of mine. What has he done?" I told him what was going on and that Parisian most likely isn't going to do anything. He said, "He is in the Steak and Shake behind you. I will have him meet you at his car. He will owe me big."

I called loss prevention and told them the suspect was going to meet me at his car. He told me he talked to his boss and wouldn't be able to make an arrest. I called mall security to have them meet us also, so I could at least ban him from the property and he would have a trespass warning on file. If he returned he would be arrested for trespassing.

The suspect showed up a few minutes later. He unlocked the car, and I found several thousand dollars worth of clothing from five other stores, as well as Parisian. I told him mall security was going to trespass him from the mall indefinitely. He said, "Are you serious? He didn't tell me this was going to happen." I said, "Be glad I'm not arresting you. The value of the clothing makes it a felony. If you want to keep talking, I'll put you in jail anyway. You owe him a good bust; I can do a warrant later if you keep bumping your gums." He quit talking. I said, "If you come on the mall's property, you will go straight to jail no matter who you call." He got in his car and left.

One afternoon Parisian called and reported a guy was walking out of the store with some clothing. Jeff and I were close by and got the guy as he was getting in the passenger side of a vehicle. I contacted the driver and ordered him to shut the vehicle off and give me the keys. Jeff attempted to get the suspect out, but he pulled away from him. Jeff grabbed the suspect again, but he refused to get out. I took out my pepper spray and sprayed him in the face. That seemed to make him mad. Jeff ordered him out again, but he didn't move; I sprayed him again. The suspect jumped out of the car and threw a punch at Jeff.

Jeff and I both tried to grab him, but he was so sweaty, we couldn't hold him. He pulled away from us and got into a brief fist fight with Jeff. Jeff stumbled as the suspect took off on foot; I jumped in my

Darrell McMann

cruiser. The suspect scaled the fence between the mall and a wooded area near a bowling alley. I drove around to the entrance of the bowling alley and set up a perimeter. A K9 unit responded and found the suspect within minutes. The K9 officer released his dog when the suspect refused to obey his commands. The suspect picked the dog up by the back of the neck as it was trying to bite him; I struck him several times on the legs with my Asp. He let go of the dog and dropped to his knees with his hands behind his back. All that for a $20 shirt. He was high on crack when he went in the store.

Jeff and I were walking toward the food court one afternoon to get something to eat when he saw a guy who he thought had been banned from the mall. The guy walked into a furniture store at the entrance to the food court. Mall security has pictures of people who have been trespassed in the security office. He said he was going to the office to look through the pictures. I told him I would hang around and keep an eye on him until I heard from him.

The guy walked out of the store at a brisk pace about a minute later. I was about to follow him when the store manager walked out, saw me, and yelled, "He just threw a gun!" A security guard was walking by, and I said, "Go in the store and keep an eye on the gun but don't touch it." I caught up to the suspect as he was about to walk out of the mall. Not knowing if he had a second gun I confronted him at gunpoint at the mall doors and at the entrance to Ruby Tuesday; everyone ran except for the suspect. I escorted the suspect back to the security office, where we discovered he was who Jeff thought he was.

The suspect recognized Jeff when he saw him in the food court and immediately entered the store. He was afraid we were going to confront him so he didn't want to be caught holding a gun. He walked to the back of the store. If he had slid the gun under some furniture or hid it calmly, he would have probably not been confronted. He went to the back of the store removed the gun from his waistband and tossed it onto a bookshelf. It knocked everything off the shelf, fell on a bed, and then bounced off the bed onto the floor. The employees couldn't help but notice something was happening.

Move Along; Nothing to See Here

Jeff and I rode through the parking lots around the mall every so often and randomly ran license plates on our in car computers. I was backing into my parking space when Jeff said, "That car is stolen." I said, "No, it isn't." He said, "Yes, it is," and turned the screen so I could see it. I said, "You're right." He pointed to the parking lot and said, "There it is—they're parking." We contacted them as they were about to walk into the food court. My guy did as I asked, but Jeff's ran into the mall. I patted my guy down real quickly, cuffed him, and put him in the backseat of my cruiser.

Jeff was chasing his guy through the mall—they ran through Dillards; with my guy in the backseat, I drove in the direction the suspect was running and was able to cut the suspect off when he ran out into the parking lot. The suspect was a juvenile who had run away from home, taking his mother's car. The passenger just happened to be with him when we saw the car. The passenger said, "This is the first time I have been stopped by the police that I wasn't messin' up."

One morning I heard dispatch put out a call for a traffic crash at Ninth and Bayou. I was about to tell dispatch that I would take it, when a motorcycle officer advised he would take it. My sergeant called me on the radio and asked me to call him at the office. I called him, and he said, "Did you hear the call at Ninth and Bayou?" I said, "Yes." He said, "You know you can leave the mall to take calls." I said, "Yes sir, I know and I do." He said, "THEN WHY DIDN'T YOU TAKE THAT CALL?" I said, "A motor officer was on top of it and took it." He said, "OH!" and hung up.

A few minutes later, dispatch put out a disturbance at Target across the street. Two patrol units were close by and took it; my cell phone rang, and it was the sergeant. "DAMMIT! WHY DIDN'T YOU TAKE THAT CALL?" I said, "Two patrol units were right down the street. He said, "WHAT THE HELL ARE YOU DOING?" I said, "I'm watching a guy we had problems with last week." He said, "YOU KNOW DAMMIT…, I hung up.

My cell phone rang, and the sergeant said, "I know you didn't just hang up on me." I said, "What do you need, Sarge?" He said, "Why haven't you signed the payroll." I said, "I did." He said, "NO THE HELL…"

Darrell McMann

I hung up and told myself I was going to drive downtown and shoot him in the head if he yelled at me again. When my cell phone rang again, I was walking to my cruiser. The sergeant said, "Yeah, I missed your signature on the payroll. Are you by yourself today?" He knew I was, but I said, "Yes sir, I'm alone today." He said, "Okay. See ya."

The sergeant would yell at Ski, Jeff, and I for things we didn't do and had no idea what he was talking about. Ski called me one morning and said, "Hey, Sarge wants us to meet with him in the office for a talk." I said, "OH, YEAH, WE ARE GOING TO TALK ALL RIGHT!" I called Jeff and told him. We were fired up when we walked in his office. He asked us to close the door. He leaned back in his chair with his hands clasped behind his head and said, "I just want you guys to know I think ya'll are doing a fantastic job up there." He started praising us because he never got any complaints about us. I felt like someone punched me in the stomach. I looked at Ski and Jeff, and they both had looks of complete disbelief on their faces. We walked out and felt like we were cheated.

Jeff and I were working one night when we heard patrol was involved in a vehicle pursuit, and the chase was heading toward the mall. The suspect turned into the entrance to the mall followed by two cruisers. We joined the chase as it continued on the service road around the mall. The suspect left the parking lot and eventually headed west on Langley Avenue. We continued west on Airport Boulevard. The suspect entered a residential area that led to Airport Boulevard, so we decided to wait for him. He changed course and headed back to the mall. We blocked traffic at Ninth and Airport and waited on the suspect; when he turned back into the mall and drove the outskirts of the parking lot along Ninth Avenue, we positioned our cruiser on Ninth Avenue so that we were parallel to his car. The suspect turned north and sped up. He struck a median on the south side of Regions Bank and went airborne back onto Ninth Avenue. Then he turned west on Airport Boulevard followed by the two cruisers that initiated the chase and us. The departments chase policy states that only two cruisers can be involved in a chase, along with a supervisor; everyone else is required to remain parallel to the vehicles involved in the chase.

Move Along; Nothing to See Here

We were on Airport approaching Highway 29 when a sergeant asked the second unit how many cruisers were involved in the chase. I shut everything down and turned around. The officer said, "Two."

We headed back to the mall. The suspect made several turns and was headed back to the mall. Jeff said, "Get me to my car—you can't have all the fun." I said, "We don't have time." The suspect was T-boned at an intersection on Davis Highway a few minutes later.

Parisian notified us they were having a problem with a guy sitting on a chair between the double doors of the main entrance of the store exposing himself to women as they entered the store. He was positioned in a way that the cameras couldn't see him. He was doing it at the same time every day. They were going to have an employee keep an eye on the area and would call us if he was there.

A few days later the suspect returned. He was in the act of exposing himself when they attempted to confront him. He ran out of the store and scaled the fence behind the bowling alley. I was on Airport Boulevard when they called. I drove to the edge of the wooded area and got out of my cruiser. I heard him running through the woods and decided I would wait for him. He turned the corner and came to a stop when he saw me. I ordered him to the ground and cuffed him. I stood him up and he said, "Officer, someone was chasing me through the woods." I said, "Why were they chasing you through the woods?" He wasn't expecting that question and paused for about fifteen seconds. I said, "You were not being chased through the woods." He said, "How do you know that?" I said, "They didn't follow you. They told us where you were last seen." He didn't say anything else. I thought I recognized him and asked him if I had arrested him before, but he didn't answer me. I checked his name and remembered I had arrested him downtown in an office building. He had snuck into the women's restroom and hid in a stall. He would masturbate while watching women in the bathroom.

The mall hired extra officers for Friday and Saturday nights because of the large crowds of teenagers that showed up and caused problems. That was typical, but I wasn't expecting trouble to come from one of my fellow officers.

John Candy and I went to a nearby restaurant for dinner before the crowds showed up. It was a Saturday night in July. We finished eating and went to the register to pay. I paid first and handed him my keys. I had to use the restroom and told him I would be out in a minute. I came out a few minutes later and found John in the driver seat of my cruiser. He said, "I'll drive." I shrugged my shoulders and got in the passenger side. I really didn't think anything could happen.

We headed back to the mall down Twelfth Avenue, turned onto Airport Boulevard, and then turned into the mall entrance. When he hit the parking lot it happened. He stomped on the accelerator and started doing figure eights in the parking lot between Parisian and Best Buy. I was so shocked I couldn't say anything for a minute. He was laughing. I yelled, "WHAT IN THE HELL ARE YOU DOING?" He was laughing when he said, "I'm checking your brakes." I yelled, "STOP THE DAMN CAR!" He stopped. I said, "Don't you realize where we are? We are at the busiest place in town on a nice summer night. People are everywhere. What the hell is wrong with you?" He laughed. I said, "I want you to go park, don't go over fifteen miles per hour, and don't check my brakes." He parked and I said, "Give me my keys." He gave them to me and asked, "Where are you going?" I said, "Away from you." Ski fired him from working off duty at the mall a couple days later.

One Saturday night, while waiting for the teens to show up, I was leaning against my cruiser "chillaxin" near the food court entrance. I couldn't believe how many parents dropped their kids off, some as young as ten-years-old, and left. I felt like I was babysitting, but that drove the point home. I started noticing teen girls, as young as thirteen- and fourteen-years-old, walk in with backpacks, and walk straight to the bathroom. They would come out a few minutes later looking older and additionally blessed.

Taxi cab drivers were a huge headache. They were always arguing over fares. They had several designated parking spaces in the food court parking lot that caused problems because they would argue over the spaces. Two drivers that drove for the same company had a disagreement over a fare one afternoon. Driver one felt like driver two stole his fare. Driver one approached Driver two and voiced his displeasure. Driver two told Driver one to get out of his face before he knocked him out. Driver one called Driver two a prick. Driver two punched Driver one breaking his nose. Driver one, aka the victim, called 911. The victim had several witnesses who were also cab drivers. I called the taxi cab company and asked them to send Driver two back to the mall. He showed up a few minutes later and I arrested him. The victim started taunting the suspect as I put him in my cruiser. I said, "I wouldn't do that if I were you. He already smacked you around pretty good. Do you think it's wise to give him another reason to beat you down again?" He shut his mouth and walked away. The suspect said, "It's too late. I'm going to beat him down again."

The next night a cab driver approached me. She wanted to complain about other drivers. I opened my door and grabbed a binder. I said, "Do you see this?" She said, "Yes, what is it?" I said, "It's the city ordinance covering taxi cabs. I think I am going to begin to strictly enforce it. I really like the section addressing personal appearance." I looked at her and said, "Let's see what I can find wrong with you. You are wearing sandals; you can't wear open-toed shoes. You are supposed to be wearing your driver ID tag on a lanyard around your neck." I looked over at the driver she had been talking to. I said, "Drivers are supposed to present a professional appearance. His shirt is not tucked in, and it's only buttoned halfway. I'm sick and tired of dealing with ya'll. I feel like I'm babysitting. Should I inspect your cabs?" She said, "No." I said, "I suggest you let everyone know we are tired of dealing with ya'll. If you have a legitimate non whiney complaint, we will be more than happy to investigate." She walked away. I didn't have any problems with cab drivers for a couple of months.

Elizabeth had started feeling guilty because she couldn't remember anything about Kim. I told her a few things, but it didn't help her. Cindy and I finally talked her into going to see Kim's headstone. Cindy bought some flowers, and we made the trip to the cemetery on April 5, 2003.

Darrell McMann

On April 8, I came home from work, and the phone was ringing, so I answered it. A young girl asked for Elizabeth, and I thought it was someone Elizabeth went to school with, so I handed her the phone. I went to the bedroom to change.

Cindy overheard Elizabeth talking on the phone. She heard her give some answers to questions that a kid she went to school with shouldn't have to ask. Cindy asked Elizabeth who was on the phone, and she said, "It's my cousin." Cindy gave me the phone, and I asked who it was, but she hung up on me. Elizabeth told me she heard someone in the background coaching the little girl on what questions to ask. I checked the caller ID, called the number, and asked for Kim's sister. I told her that if she wanted to know something, she needed to ask me. She said that didn't know what I was talking about. I told her not to call my house ever again and hung up.

I thought about it for a couple of days and decided I couldn't let it go so easily so I called her. I told her if she wanted to talk to me, she could meet me somewhere on my off day. We decided we would meet at the Taco Bell in the afternoon in Brewton on the 17th.

We met at the Taco Bell, and I decided I would let her speak first. Instead of trying to make things right, she continued the attacks on Kim. She said, "Kim lied about everything, she was rebellious, she was running from demons, and she didn't know what she was doing when she got saved." I asked, "Are you finished?" She nodded yes. I said, "You forgot to mention that she was a lesbian. I found out a couple of things since we last spoke, and I have a few questions for you."

I said, "There was incident at the hospital in Brewton that involved a misunderstanding between the staff and the husband of a patient. Kim was worried and asked if I could keep Elizabeth that night. I told her I had to be at work at 5:00 A.M. I asked what was going on. She told me she might have to work late but would just work at home. We talked for a minute, but she didn't tell me what happened. Kim called your mother and explained what happened, and asked if ya'll could come get Elizabeth. Ya'll refused to help her. Thankfully the issue was

155

Move Along; Nothing to See Here

cleared up that night. Why didn't ya'll help her?" She couldn't answer. I continued, "When Kim left Elizabeth with your parents on weekends when we both worked, your mother charged her $100. If I had known that at the time, other arrangements would have been made." Her response? Kim was lying.

She repeated her accusation that I'd had an affair with Tina, and I countered by pointing out that I didn't even like her because she was whiney and needy. "Kim thought so too and was about to ask her to leave the house." Her sister said, "Kim was going to ask her to leave because she was a lesbian." I said, "If we were having an affair, that would make her bisexual." I guess I caught her and she realized it, so she gave that argument a rest.

"If ya'll really wanted to see Elizabeth, you wouldn't try to be sneaky about it," I said. "Ya'll have never sent her a Christmas or a birthday card. You would rather be sneaky. One of you mentioned someone overheard my parents tell me to get Elizabeth away from your parents. Who overheard that conversation? Did I ever do or say anything to lead any of you to believe that I wasn't going to allow ya'll to see Elizabeth?" She said, "I don't know who overheard it, but I know it happened. I can't think of anything right now that made any of us think you wouldn't allow us to see Elizabeth, but I'm sure something happened to make us think that."

I said, "You nor any member or friend of your family will call my house." She said, "Are you going to change your number?" I said, "No, I'm not going to change my number because you will forget the number. I have put up with you and your family's trash long enough. If I have to put you in jail to prove my point, then that's what I will do. Things could have worked out from the beginning, but ya'll wouldn't let it happen. I am done." I left and drove home.

I transferred back to patrol on the day shift after a year at the mall. I enjoyed the assignment, but we had a lot of downtime. I got tired of walking through the mall and dealing teenagers on the weekends.

Darrell McMann

The City of Pensacola has numerous historical sights downtown for tourists. One of them is an old locomotive surrounded by a wrought iron fence in the median on Garden Street. A citizen called one Sunday around midmorning to say that a guy had climbed the fence and was throwing paint cans from the train onto Garden Street. When I showed up, I noticed there were several paint cans in the westbound lanes. I saw someone standing in the cab of the train. I asked, "What's going on?" He said, "I want the Pensacola News Journal to come and interview me." I said, "Why don't you come down here and talk to me." He said, "I ain't coming down, and you can't get me down." I started to climb over the fence, which is about three feet high, two feet from the train, and five feet below the cab of the train. When I got one leg over the fence, he said, "Hey officer." I looked up and saw that he had a butcher knife in his hand. I thought about it a minute. I couldn't justify shooting him if he warned me. I also couldn't justify shooting him if all I had to do was throw my leg back over the fence. I decided to throw my leg back over the fence.

Sergeant Tent showed up and asked, "Why is he still on that train?" I looked up at the guy and said, "Hey, show him why you are still on the train." He showed the knife; then he threw me a letter that he claimed proved there was a government conspiracy against him. He demanded to be interviewed. Sarge called for SWAT, and we shut down a few blocks of Garden Street.

Sometime after we closed the street down, he got a rope out of his backpack and tied it to the smoke stack of the train. The crisis negotiators tried to talk to him for several hours, but he was adamant about being interviewed. He must have decided he wasn't getting anywhere, so he placed the noose around his neck and jumped off the top of the train. He didn't plan well—the rope had too much slack in it, and he was yanked backwards into the side of the train. He fell to the ground with the wind knocked out of him. He was taken to the hospital and Baker Acted. The Baker Act is an involuntary seventy two hour mental examination in the state of Florida

Move Along; Nothing to See Here

Cindy won a trip to Disney World through work. We drove down in May and stayed at one of the resorts. The three of us had a blast. On our last day, we were at one of the parks waiting in line at one of the restaurants to order lunch. There were eight lines with at least ten people in each line. There were three sixteen- to eighteen-year-old males in the line to my left. They were horsing around and talking loudly. One of them was pushed into me and started cursing. I said, "Hey, ya'll need to watch your language and quit messing around because there are young kids around." One of them turned around and said, "Who are you? What are you going to do?" I said, "You keep bumping your gums, and you will find out." His buddy grabbed him and told him to calm down. Meanwhile, Cindy told Elizabeth to go find us a table.

A few minutes later the mouthy kid turned around and looked at me. He said, "Who are you looking at?" I said, "I'm looking at you!" He asked if I wanted to go outside. Before I could answer, I felt a heavy hand on my shoulder. I turned around to face a man about my age, but he was about two inches shorter but about two feet thicker. He said, "Are these guys giving you problems?" I said, "Yes, they are." He said, "Do you need some help?" I said, "I guess I could use some help." He looked at the guys and said, "Hey, where are you idiots from?" One of them said, "Philadelphia, PA!" He said, "I'm from Philly, too. Me and this man are about to beat some ass in Disney. When I get back to Philly, I'll find the three of ya and beat the hell out of ya in Philly, too!" One them said, "I'm a juvenile." He said, "Do we look like we care?" They turned around and didn't say anything else.

I turned around to talk to my tag-team partner, but he had walked away. I was still pretty aggravated; there were at least five other fathers within ten feet of me with toddlers who saw what was going on and had to keep moving their kids to keep them from being bumped into by the idiots. They never said a word.

Chapter 15

In May of 2004, I was selected to be one of the departments FTOs on the evening shift. The PPD has four FTOs assigned to the evening shift and four FTOs assigned to the midnight shift. We were all on the same squad. Day shift would start a FTO squad about a year later.

My first trainee was Damon Wayons. One of our first calls was for a disturbance at Tom Ann and Buddy's, which is a hole-in-the-wall bar on West Cervantes Street. When we pulled into the parking lot, a black female ran up to my cruiser and pointed at a black male running through the vacant lot across Cervantes Street. She was very drunk and told us he was her boyfriend and had assaulted her. She had scratches on her neck and face. One side of her face was slightly swollen and her nose was bleeding. He had circled the block on a bicycle that someone left on the side of the road. We caught up to him directly across the street from the bar; he was extremely drunk, too. I told the boyfriend he was under arrest; he turned around when I tried to cuff him. I spun him around onto the hood of my cruiser and forced one of his arms behind his head. We cuffed him after a brief struggle.

The boyfriend was telling us jokes and having a normal conversation with us until I stopped at the door to the sally port of the jail. I was informed by the detention officer working the security camera the sally port was full. He told me to park in one of the parking spaces in the driveway, and he would buzz the door open when we wanted to come in. As I was backing up, the boyfriend said, "I ain't going in there. You are going to have to kill me." As an officer with fourteen years' experience, I had heard that many times and nothing had ever happened. We parked the cruiser and secured our weapons in the trunk. I opened the back door and said, "Come on, let's go." He said, "I told you I ain't goin'!" I grabbed his shirt and pulled him out. I started walking toward the door, and he turned toward me and tried to head butt me. I blocked it and turned him around. I grabbed his cuffed wrists

Move Along; Nothing to See Here

and forced them as high as they could go. We walked to the sally port door and I held him against the wall until the door was buzzed open.

When the sally port door opened, he pushed backward, causing me to stumble. Damon grabbed him and took him through the door. He turned toward me as I came through the door behind them. Damon turned him around. He started hopping like a rabbit in the sally port. Damon was trying to lead him to the door to enter the receiving area of the jail. The boyfriends hopping caused Damon to stumble; the boyfriend happened to be in midair when Damon stumbled. The boyfriend's face met the rear windshield of a Florida Highway Patrol State Trooper cruiser; the entire rear windshield shattered which startled the trooper who was in his cruiser completing a report.

The trooper and I had attended a couple of training courses together. He got out of his cruiser and said, "Hey, I haven't seen you in a while, how are ya?" I said, "Just fine how about you?" Meanwhile Damon is yelling, "Hey, he's knocked out. What do I do?" I said put him on the floor. He laid him on the floor and yelled, "He is bleeding!" I told him I could see that and called for an ambulance and a supervisor. I notified the jail nurse who administered first aid. The trooper said, "I've been wanting a new cruiser—maybe I can get one now." We spoke for a few minutes while Damon was freaking out. I told him to calm down. I could tell the cut wasn't too bad and that we didn't do anything wrong. Everything in the sally port and what happened outside would be on video.

One of our sergeants met us, and I told him what happened; he went to view the video; Damon was still panicking. The jail nurse cleaned up the boyfriend and told me she could take care of him. We didn't need to take him to the hospital. The sergeant walked back out to meet us and told me the video backed up what I had told him. He looked at Damon and said, "Don't throw anyone else through a car if you can help it." When he walked out, Damon was still panicking. I told him to calm down. I said, "The only one who made a mistake was me. I should have told the deputy our guy was probably going to fight. They would have let me drive in. A couple of correction

Darrell McMann

deputies would have come out to get him and then we could have parked outside. Learn from my mistake."

Damon wanted to work and accepted constructive criticism well. He enjoyed making citizen contacts and striking up conversations with them. We were on Cervantes one night when we passed a prostitute walking along wearing a very short black miniskirt. He said, "I'm getting out with her." He turned around, stopped on a side street, and called her over to him. I knew this was going to be interesting—she didn't like talking to the police; didn't have front teeth, which was a positive attribute for her profession; and didn't wear panties. She would raise her skirt to passing cars for advertisement.

Damon approached her and she said, "What you want? I ain't done nothing." He said, "I'm new and I just wanted to meet you." She said, "I don't give a damn if you new or old. I don't want to know you." Damon pointed at me and said, "You see him?" She said, "Yeah I see him, and I know him, but I don't want to talk to him either." He said, "He is my training officer and I gotta make a good impression." She said, "What do you think he will say about this." She raised her skirt— no panties—and directed a few pelvic thrusts at Damon; she turned around to display her backside and walked away. He said, "OH LAWD, WHAT HAPPENED? HEY, WHAT'S YOUR NAME?" She didn't answer him. He said, "I gotta name for you—NO DRAWERS!" She turned and gave him a brief glimpse of what he was missing.

We answered a disturbance call at the Backseat Lounge one night. The Backseat was a strip bar. We were standing in the lobby speaking to the manager and several customers when one of the dancers came in to join the conversation. She was topless, and Damon's attention shifted to her two friends. I said, "Hey, haven't you ever seen any before? You have kids." He said, "Yeah, but not like those."

My son Trip was born on July 11, 2004—another very proud day for me. It's an awesome feeling to be present when your child is born. It's an emotionally draining experience that I wouldn't trade for anything.

161

Move Along; Nothing to See Here

September 15, 2004 we reported for duty not knowing what to expect. Hurricane Ivan was churning through the Gulf of Mexico as a strong category three hurricane. The last bad hurricane I experienced was Frederick in 1979. We had several category ones and twos since 1979 but nothing too bad. At dusk my new trainee and I were riding through Sanders Beach, when I pulled into the boat launch parking lot at the dead end of South K Street; I didn't get very far. We had white caps in the parking lot. I thought to myself, "This isn't going to be good." The storm wasn't going to make landfall for another five or six hours. The last building I saw before the sun went down was an apartment building at the dead end of South I Street. There was nothing left but the slab the next day.

At about midnight the wind was approaching sustained hurricane strength of seventy-four miles per hour. It was getting difficult to drive because of the wind and flying debris. Transformers were blowing up, and they gave the sky an eerie bluish glow. Around 12:30 A.M. the chief called everyone off the street. The sustained wind strength would eventually reach 130 miles per hour.

When we got to the police department I placed my sleeping bag behind a desk in the records department. The chief had the desk sergeant make an announcement that anyone leaving the building had to sign out. A couple officers left but came back a few minutes later.

I was lying on the floor when I realized the building was shaking from the wind. It sounded like a train was passing within a few feet of the building. I joined several officers in the desk sergeant's office (DSO) to watch the news. Around 2:00 a.m., when the storm was really kicking, a lieutenant got on the radio and advised that he was at Summit and Scenic Highway with a DUI. Everyone in DSO said, "What the hell is he doing? What an idiot." They were referring to the lieutenant not the DUI. There were several other more disparaging remarks about his mental capacity. The lieutenant asked for a unit to transport the DUI; everyone in DSO was quiet. We were waiting to see if anyone was going to volunteer. Someone did. An officer who was across town on Navy Boulevard spoke up and volunteered to go get him.

Darrell McMann

There were several disparaging remarks made about his mental capacity also. I went back to records and lay down.

About 7:00 A.M. an announcement was made for the shifts to have a lineup in different parts of the building. Our lieutenant told us we would be working twelve-hour shifts 7:00 A.M. to 7:00 P.M. with no off days until further notice. He told us we could go home but to be prepared to leave early enough to get back in time. If it takes you two hours to get home, then be prepared for it to take you two hours to get back here tonight.

I usually took interstate I110 north home. The first unit that tried to go north on the interstate didn't see the low-hanging power line. Her light bar was ripped from the top of her cruiser. She got out picked it up and threw it in her backseat. I decided to use Palafox.

I could see damaged buildings and uprooted trees everywhere; debris and power lines were all over the road. For the most part, Palafox/highway 29 was clear. When I turned unto Ten Mile Road, I had to turn around due to downed trees. I drove south to 9 ½ Mile Road but had to turn around after a few blocks because of downed trees. I decided to try Nine Mile Road for an open route. Cove Road was passable, and I was able to drive around several trees, until I got to Nine and One-Half Mile Road. Downed trees blocked Cove, so I turned west and went to the next street. I met a deputy heading east. We looked up the street and noticed it looked clear except for a downed tree. I don't know where the deputy spent the night, but he looked wild eyed and was talking ninety to nothing. He said, "Come on, we can get through there!" He drove around the tree into a shallow ditch and barely got through. I had an older cruiser and knew I would get stuck because my rear end was lower than his. I turned around and headed back to Nine Mile Road.

Since it was now obvious that I couldn't get to my house, I decided to try and get to Cindy's parents house, which is where Cindy and the kids had spent the night. That plan looked like it would have to be scrapped when I encountered several downed trees blocking the

Move Along; Nothing to See Here

road. I was about to turn around and go back downtown when two pickup trucks went around me. Four guys got out and started cutting a path through the trees. I followed them all the way to Pine Forest Road, which was somewhat passable. I had to go off road a few times and had to watch the power lines. I had to wait a couple of times for the wind to blow the lines high enough for me to pass beneath them. I didn't want a power line to get snagged by my light bar.

I managed to get all the way to West Roberts, which was clear all the way to Cindy's parents' road. I turned on their road and got about halfway, when I found the road blocked by downed trees. I stopped in front of a house to assess the situation. The people who lived in the house recognized me and asked if I wanted to borrow one of their four wheelers. I said, "Sure. Do you mind if I leave the car in your drive-way?" They said no and went to get the keys. I drove up to the house a few minutes later. What was usually a twelve- to fifteen-minute ride had taken me two and one-half hours.

I walked in the house and went to sleep. Actually, I closed my eyes, but I couldn't sleep because I was worried about my house. Around noon, Cindy and I decided to try and get to the house since we knew people were out removing the trees from the roads. We were relieved to find the house had no damage. Our privacy fence took a beating and the walls of our above-ground pool had collapsed, but there was no water in it because I hadn't had time to repair a cut in the liner.

We came in for our shifts and found out several officers had either lost their homes or their homes had major damage. I felt blessed. We had a dusk-to-dawn curfew, and that made us happy. Power was out everywhere, and Gulf Power was predicting it would take three weeks to get everyone's power restored.

I was dispatched to a house that first night for a citizen assist. Two elderly females lived together in a house in the Tan Yards; they couldn't remove the plywood from their windows. It was like a sauna in the house, so I asked them for a hammer and a ladder. I went out to remove the plywood, but the ladder wasn't tall enough. I called

Darrell McMann

for the Fire Department. An engine came, and the crew removed the plywood from the windows. I went in to see if the females needed anything else, but they had both fallen asleep. There was a nice cool breeze blowing through the house. I walked outside and a female down the street asked me, "Hey, how long the power going to be out?" I said, "Gulf Power is saying three weeks." She directed her comments at some other people and said, "Did ya'll hear that?" "The M F'n police said the power is going to be out three weeks!" I thought, "Wow, don't kill the messenger."

We had very few calls and couldn't get through the neighborhoods because of all the downed trees. I kept looking up and saying, "Man, it's really dark and look at how bright the stars are.

The two FTOs on the squad with me also had new trainees. On the second night we decided to park and pick a neighborhood to walk through. Around 2:00 A.M. we parked off of Garden Street and walked into the Tan Yards neighborhood. We got to the first east-west street, Romana Street, and I heard someone walking through some tree limbs and noticed a flashlight moving back and forth along the side of a house. I stood in the intersection and watched as the person made his way out to the street. He walked toward me and got within five feet of me before realizing someone was there. He was surprised to find six police officers standing there. I asked him what he was doing, and he said, "I'm checking out my girlfriend's house." He came up with a name when I asked him what her name was. We checked the house; no one was home, and it appeared no one had tried to get in. We didn't see anyone awake or at home next door or across the street to ask who lived in the house to check his story. I told him there was a dusk–to–dawn curfew, and he could be arrested. He told me he lived down the street and wouldn't violate the curfew again. I told him I would give him the benefit of a doubt and allow him to go home. He thought he was slick, but I knew I would see him again.

The following Monday night a married couple was sitting in their car, which was parked in front of their house on West La Rua Street, listening to the Monday Night Football game on their car radio. They noticed a guy walking down the middle of the street looking at the houses as he walked by. When he got to their house, he stopped in front of their car and peered at the house, which seemed empty. He didn't notice them sitting in the car. He suddenly sprinted to the front door. He was almost in the house when the husband yelled at him from the car, "What are you doing? That's my house!" He said, "I'm looking for someone, but this ain't his house!" Then he ran back out to the street and kept walking west. The home owners decided to follow him until they could find an officer. They drove about two blocks when they flagged down a National Guard Humvee; they told them what happened. I was dispatched to assist the National Guard with a suspect.

I pulled up and noticed three soldiers were holding a guy at gunpoint in the middle of the street. The home owners told me what happened, and as I walked over, I immediately recognized the guy as the prowler from two nights before. I said, "I knew I would see you again." As you can imagine, he looked happy to see me.

About three days after the storm, a large contingent of Tennessee tree cutters came to town. They took nearly every room at the Travel Inn on Cervantes Street. The Travel Inn is definitely not a three-, four- or five-star hotel. It may not even have a ranking. I thought at the time it was kind of funny that a bunch of Tennessee rednecks were staying at a hotel in a black neighborhood.

Betsy Mims and I were parked in the Walgreens parking lot at about 4:00 A.M. Both of our trainees were off because their homes had been damaged. It was a nice cool night, so we were standing outside our cruisers talking. I think I was actually sleeping in a standing position. We thought we heard something a block or so behind us and turned toward the noise. We saw a black female, actually a transvestite, running toward us followed by about ten white males. They tackled shim and started working shim over. We ran down the street to stop them. The shim had apparently snuck into a room and stole a wallet from one of the tree cutters. His story didn't make any sense. Some of the other guys told us that shim knocked on all the doors

Darrell McMann

to see if anyone needed some company. They all said they could tell shim was not a her. The "victim" wasn't as observant and discovered the truth as they were getting to know each other. He had already paid and demanded a refund. Shim refused to give him a refund and grabbed his wallet as shim ran out. The "victim" ran after shim and screamed that he had been robbed. Several of his coworkers were outside talking and chased shim down.

The National Guard always assists cities and counties during emergencies, but it amazed me how many agencies sent officers to help us. Most of them were assigned duties during the day shift. I always made a point of thanking them when I could.

Over the summer I was selected to be a hostage negotiator on the SWAT team. The officers working the north side of the city responded to a man with a gun call in Pensacola Village. He went inside an apartment and forced a female and her child to leave. She told the officers her boyfriend was asleep in the bedroom. Thinking they had a possible hostage situation the SWAT team was called out. I dropped my trainee off with another officer and headed to the Village.

I showed up at the village and couldn't believe how many outside agencies were helping out with the perimeter, which was good because large crowds are commonplace in Pensacola Village. I was selected to attempt to make contact with the suspect. SWAT borrowed the apartment next door and had everything set up by the time I got there. When I was ready, one of the officers placed a speaker next to the front door. I talked for about forty-five minutes, and I noticed that everyone across the courtyard had opened their front doors so they could watch the show. I kept hearing someone say, "Yeah come on out. We don't want to hurt you—we just want to kill you." Someone was listening to the Roy Jones Jr. fight. We knew it when he got knocked out. Someone stepped out and yelled, "HEY, ROY JONES JUST GOT KNOCKED THE F OUT!"

I talked for another thirty minutes, and then we changed negotiators. The SWAT team broke a window to see if they could get

Move Along; Nothing to See Here

someone's attention. When they did, the "hostage" started negotiating for the suspect. It took another twenty minutes before the suspect gave himself up.

As we were walking back to our cruisers, we were notified we were needed on Langley Avenue. Officers responded to a domestic disturbance involving another gun. Kenny Charles stopped down the street and got out of his cruiser; then he heard a gun shot. The officers were speaking to the wife when the husband killed himself in the house; we were told to cancel. I headed back downtown and reclaimed my trainee. The first shot Kenny heard struck his windshield just above the windshield wiper. It grazed his steering wheel and came to a stop in the head rest of the driver seat. If he had stayed in the cruiser for a few more seconds, he would have definitely been shot.

The Backseat opened up when they got power back within a week of the storm. We went in to have them shut down in compliance with the curfew. It was the first time it rained after the hurricane, and I could see they had major roof damage. When I walked in the lobby I noticed water was dripping from several places, and it was even worse in the bar. I got disgusted when I noticed one of the girls was pole dancing underneath a large hole in the roof. There was dirt and debris all over the stage, which didn't affect her routine. Apparently it was quite alluring to a couple of guys who were intently watching her.

Betsy, Timmy Thompson, and I along with our trainees responded to Bayou Grove late one night for a disturbance. There were three houses on Fairmont that constantly fought with each other. A young gay couple lived on the corner, and two houses down was an older gay couple that stayed drunk and argued frequently. Next to them was a family that can best be described as white trash. I knew them pretty well. They drank and fought with everybody. No one had power so most everyone along the street was outside enjoying the cool weather. For the festivities on this particular night several members of the white trash family had been drinking and started arguing with the older gay couple next door that had also been drinking. The

Darrell McMann

young gay couple was sober but got mad with the white trash family for using antigay slurs. One of them had a sister who was spending the night. She got into an argument with her brother's boyfriend. She didn't like the fact that her brother was gay.

We arrested three members of the white trash family, the older gay couple, and the sister who didn't like her brother's boyfriend. When we left, it was quiet except for the young gay couple arguing in the front yard. I guess they made up because we didn't have to go back.

We worked three weeks without a day off; because of the curfew, the night shift wasn't so bad—the officers on the day shift had much more to deal with than we did. We patrolled the neighborhoods and enforced the curfew; we only had a few people who questioned the legality of a curfew. We arrested them and told them to present their case to a judge; I didn't have to appear in court for anyone I arrested for violating the curfew, I'm assuming it wasn't a violation of their civil rights. I was incredibly tired because it was next to impossible to sleep. We didn't get our power back for just over two weeks, and it was just too hot to sleep. If I dozed off, the sound of neighbors cutting up trees all day would wake me up. I wasn't complaining very loudly because I still had a house.

I'm proud that everyone at the police department worked tirelessly and without complaint. We all worked together and got through it. A group of officers got together and went around to other officers homes that had a lot of tree damage and helped them out.

I will admit we ate very well during this period. The FOP sent a refrigerated truck full of food from south Florida. When our shift came in, dinner was being served. Two officers would grill fish, hamburgers, or something else at about 2:00 A.M. Breakfast would be ready when our shift was over.

Usually by the third week with new trainees in their first phase you can pinpoint some things they need to work on. The hurricane

Move Along; Nothing to See Here

severely disrupted the process; my trainee didn't start writing reports until the fourth week.

We responded to a complicated clustered domestic complaint. He got all the information he needed and typed his report. When I checked the narrative, I noticed all the words were underlined in red, which indicated they were misspelled. I pointed this out to him, and he told me he typed fast which accounted for all the misspellings. He said he could use the spell check and fix it quickly. He actually wrote a very good report, but I still thought it was odd that every word was misspelled.

The last night he was with me we were dispatched to a shots fired call on Whispering Pines. He was driving and stopped to look at the street index. One function of an FTO requires you to put some stress on your trainees. It took longer than I thought it should to look up the street, so I asked, "You can read a map can't you?" He said, "Yes." I said, "What's taking you so long? Let's go!" Dispatch called him and told him the complainant heard another shot fired. He was still looking at the map. I said, "Didn't you hear that? More shots are being fired. LET'S GO!" He took off. I wasn't very familiar with the area, but I had a good idea where the street was.

He stopped just before we got to one of the intersecting streets. He looked at the map for a while, and I said, "LET'S GO!" He took off again and turned down the correct street. He drove for a few blocks and stopped in the middle of the street looking around. Our headlights illuminated the street sign of the street we were going to which was the next block. I asked, "What are you doing?" He said, "I can't find the street." I said, "It ain't gonna magically appear in front of you. LET'S GO!" He took off again and almost didn't see the street. He said, "Oh, there it is," and turned.

He was traveling at about fifty miles per hour down the street. I caught a couple of addresses and noticed a lot of people in their yards. When we got to the block the complainant lived on I said, "HAVE YOU SEEN ANY ADDRESSES OR ARE YOU JUST DRIVING? WE

Darrell McMann

PROBABLY DROVE RIGHT BY THE HOUSE!" He stopped. He happened to stop right in front of the neighbor's house. I immediately got out of the cruiser and found a tree to stand behind, he asked, "Where are you going?" I said, "Shots fired and you park right in front of the house—you ain't getting me killed." He joined me behind the tree. I could hear fireworks in the distance and heard a couple of bottle rockets whiz by. I saw a neighbor next door and walked over. I asked her if she heard anything strange. She said, "We have a lot of Red Sox fans who live on this street. They got excited when they won and started shooting fireworks." I thanked her. I contacted the home owner, who was an elderly female that lived alone. She thanked us for coming and thanked us again when I explained to her what she had heard. As we walked back to the cruiser he asked me, "Well how bad was it?"

I said, "That nice old lady lives alone and called for help. She thinks someone is shooting a gun. She is someone's grandmother." He hung his head. "If you can't read a map just tell me, and I will help you learn." He didn't say anything. I said, "You were cruising down the street so fast you didn't see any addresses until I said something. You didn't even know which block we were in." I said, "All the people who were outside, you could have stopped along the way and asked someone if they saw or heard anything. Then you stopped directly in front of the house. Say someone was out here with a weapon. You would most likely be dead within seconds. You should have stopped four or five houses away and approached the house quietly." He said, "So, I sucked." I said, "Yes, but tomorrow is another day. Don't do it again—learn from your many mistakes."

When he moved on to Betsy things were pretty much back to normal. He had to write more reports, which were filled with mistakes. Betsy finally got it out of him that he was dyslexic. At times we are behind by three or four reports and have to catch up. He would have a lot of problems with his disability. Unfortunately, he had to resign. I felt bad for getting on to him, but he understood.

About six weeks after Ivan, some residents who lived across from a city park in East Hill reported someone was attempting to lure

Move Along; Nothing to See Here

children into a vehicle. They gave a very good description of a vehicle but next to nothing in reference to a suspect. All the incidents were late in the afternoon around 5:00 P.M. I parked down the street the next day around 4:30 P.M. and waited. About fifteen minutes later, I was about to give up and go eat dinner, when my trainee and I observed the vehicle going east along the south side of the park. I took off to stop the vehicle. When I turned onto the street, we didn't see it. We found it parked in a driveway about two blocks east of the park. We contacted a Hispanic male on the porch and seven more in the house. They all claimed they didn't speak English, and we didn't have any Spanish-speaking officers on duty. We took pictures of all of them and checked their IDs. They all had Mexican driver's licenses. I was sure they were fake. I was also sure they understood more English than they let on. I handed one of them his license back and quickly said, "Thanks, man." He said, "You wel." He stopped himself before he could finish. We didn't have a description of the suspect, so we couldn't hold anyone. We didn't have any further complaints about someone trying to lure children. Obviously it was one of them.

November of 2004 was a huge pain. The presidential election was hot and heavy. I responded to a complaint one night of a stolen John Kerry sign. The lady was going on and on about how terrible it was that someone stole her John Kerry sign. She looked at me after a few minutes and said, "You don't even care do you?" I asked, "Is it that obvious?" She said, "Yes, you must be a Republican." I said, "I am a registered Republican, but I think they are all corrupt. You are right—I don't care, and I would have the same response if you had George Bush signs in your yard." She said, "I would like a report for theft." I said, "I'm not writing a report because the signs were paid for by some other party and given to you to display on your property. The actual owner would have to report it stolen. What I will do is write an intel report, which will be read out at all our lineups." She said, "Okay, well thank you. Sorry I wasted your time." I said, "No ma'am, nothing is ever a waste of time." She said, "You are a terrible liar." I said, "Yes ma'am."

Chapter 16

July 10, 2005 we were preparing for the arrival of Hurricane Dennis—less than a year after Hurricane Ivan. I had to get special permission to report two hours later for work, so I could be at Trip's first birthday party. This time the storm made landfall east of Pensacola. The storm wasn't nearly as large as Ivan and was over within a few hours. We still got sustained winds of over 100 miles per hour, but it was nothing like Ivan.

The day after the storm, I somehow managed to get pink eye. I went to the only pharmacy that was open, which was in Walmart on my way to work. I asked the pharmacist if there was anything over the counter that was good for pink eye, but he wasn't much help. While finishing my conversation with the pharmacist, I was tapped on the shoulder.

I turned around and was asked by a very grumpy old man, "You ain't going to do anything about those kids?" I asked, "What kids?" He said, "If I have to tell you, it ain't worth it." I said, "Obviously I have no idea what you are talking about. What kids are you talking about, and what are they doing?" He seemed aggravated that I didn't know what he was talking about. He said, "YOU DIDN'T SEE THEM RUNNING THROUGH THE STORE ALMOST KNOCKING PEOPLE DOWN?" I said, "APPARENTLY not, because I had to ask YOU what YOU are talking about." His wife walked up and said, "It's okay. They were running out when we came in twenty minutes ago." I said, "Really now that explains why I had no idea what you are talking about. I've been here five minutes, so they were gone fifteen minutes before I got here." He grumbled and walked away. I wanted to do more than grumble, but I bit my tongue and went to work.

We worked twelve-hour shifts again but for only a week. I had a trainee, Eddie Griffin, during this storm. He had to ride with another

Move Along; Nothing to See Here

FTO for two days while I got rid of my pink eye. He was a good kid with a big heart, but he had poor judgment. He got through FTO okay, but he had to resign about six months later because of decisions he had made.

Eddie was driving and stopped for the red light at Pace and Cervantes at about 3:00 A.M. A vehicle came to a stop next to us on his side. He motioned for the driver to roll his window down. When he did, Eddie yelled, "CURFEW. GO HOME!" I sat up and looked at the driver. I said to Eddie, "Hey genius, do you know who that is?" He said, "No." I said, "It's Dan Shugart from the Channel 3 News, the sports director. I bet he's on his way home." He grunted.

Three years later Dan Shugart was the guest speaker at Ransom Middle School. Elizabeth and several other students were chosen to be members of the Honor Society. I asked him if he remembered his brush with the law that night. He told me he did because he couldn't understand what Eddie said. He noticed someone lean up in the passenger seat and could tell we were having a conversation. He laughed when I told him what I said.

I backed two rookies one night on a disturbance. The girlfriend hit the boyfriend with a two-by-four several times across his head, face, and back. One side of his face was swollen, and his nose was bleeding. He had some deep scratch marks on his chest from her fingernails. She also broke all the windows and mirrors of his vehicle with the two-by-four.

The rookie assigned to the call didn't want to do a report. His rationale was the guy couldn't make up his mind if he wanted to make a report, and he wanted to talk to his mom. He said, "This is a waste of time." I said, "I think you need to think about it." He actually asked me why. I said, "Well, first of all, it's a domestic. They are dating and have a child in common. She has beaten the crap out of him and committed felony criminal mischief on his car. You don't know what condition she is in—she could be lying dead somewhere. What are you going to tell the sergeant a week from now when someone comes looking

Darrell McMann

for a report? When they ask me about it, I'm going to say I thought he wrote a report. I will be off the hook, but you won't." I left.

I responded to the Travel Inn for an anonymous complaint about a prostitute that was going in and out of a room. The caller reported there were two black males in the room but they had not come out. I went to the room and listened before knocking on the door; I couldn't hear anything, so I knocked. A black male opened the door, and I recognized him but didn't know from where. I could tell by the look on his face that he recognized me, too. I knew I had never arrested him or had contact with him as an officer. He had been sleeping, and the other black male was sawing logs.

I explained to him why I was there. He assured me that no prostitute had been in his room; he said it was just he and his friend. I talked to him for a few minutes while I gave a quick look around the room. I noticed several empty beer bottles and an empty bottle of vodka. He tried to wake his buddy up, but he was pretty wasted and wouldn't wake up. He handed me his ID and his friend's ID. When I looked at the ID and saw his name I said, "I knew I recognized you. We went to high school together." He said, "Yeah, I thought we did." I said, "We had our twentieth year reunion last June, but I didn't see you." He said, "Yeah, I couldn't make it. I was in prison." I said, "That's too bad. I hope your doing good." He said, "Yeah, I think I've turned my life around." I ran their names, but they didn't have any warrants. As I was reaching for the door, I said, "Good luck." Before I could open the door, it was opened from the outside, and a white female walked in. I turned around; he smiled and said, "You got me." I nodded and asked the female to come outside.

She was wearing a black bikini top, blue spandex shorts, and no shoes. She had a beer in her hand. She said, "I normally don't drink, but I'm celebrating." I said, "Oh yeah? What are you celebrating?" She must have forgotten what she told me because she said, "Look at my spider bite." She showed me her right ankle, which was red and swollen, and looked like it was close to oozing. She said, "Does it look infected to you?" I said, "Yeah, it does. You need to go see a doctor." Then I said,

175

Move Along; Nothing to See Here

"So, what are you celebrating?" She said, "Do you think my friends are nice?" I said, "Yes, I went to high school with one of them." She said, "That is so awesome." I asked her for her ID. She said, "So where did ya'll go to high school." I said, "So, what are you celebrating, and I need your ID." She said, "My birthday is today, I'm twenty-two." She reached into her shorts—not her pockets—and pulled out her ID. She said, "I don't think I'm wanted anywhere." She wasn't. She told me she was originally from Texas but had been living in New Orleans. She hooked up with some friends and came to Pensacola Beach.

I asked, "Where are the friends you came to town with?" She shrugged and said, "I don't know. I met your friends at a club last night, and we've been celebrating my birthday." I said, "The reason I'm here is because someone called about you. They think you are a prostitute." She said, "That's kind of funny." I asked why. She said, "I have actually prostituted before." I said, "That's just crazy. I would have never guessed." She said, "I know, right." I said, "Are you prostituting now?" She said, "Not really. I need a ride back to New Orleans, and your friend is going to Houston." I said, "So at this moment your off duty?" She said, "Yes." I asked, "Why have you been in and out of the room." She said, "I just like to walk around sometimes, but I'm not prostituting." I said, "Okay." I left and didn't see her again.

Deric Houston and I responded to a disturbance at an upstairs garage apartment. We approached the door and noticed blood on the floor by the door, blood going up the steps, and along the walls. We drew our guns, and I yelled, "Police! Anyone here?" We made our way up the stairs. We came to the door to the apartment, and it was slightly ajar. I yelled, "Police! Is anyone in the room?" We heard someone crying, and I slowly eased the door open. We saw two men sitting on a bed crying and covered in blood. We knew one of them—Keith Brocker, who was sometimes homeless but always drunk. He had more than likely dealt with every PPD officer at least once. He had also more than likely threatened every officer or fought with them. Keith had befriended another transient. Keith is bisexual and so was his new friend. Keith told us he invited his new friend to the gay Indian's apartment. He thought his new friend and the gay Indian would

Darrell McMann

hit it off. They started drinking, and Keith's Indian friend began to talk about his former life partner who died from Aids. Keith's new friend tried to cheer him up by dropping his pants and displaying the pair of women's panties he was wearing.

The gay Indian was impressed, so he dropped his pants to display the pair of women's panties he was wearing. Keith's new friend started laughing because his panties were pink and had some type of design on them that he thought was girly. The gay Indian got extremely upset that he was laughing at his panties. He informed him they were his dead life partner's panties, and he wears them to remember him. Keith told his new friend to apologize to the gay Indian. By the way, Keith addresses his gay friend as "gay Indian." Anyway, Keith's knew friend sucker punched Keith and the gay Indian. They ended up on the bed with Keith and the gay Indian fighting Keith's new friend. I noticed that the top portion of one of Keith's ears was missing, so I asked him, "Keith what happened to your ear?" He said, "The gay Indian bit me by mistake." I realized the gay Indian hadn't said anything. I looked at him, and he started to cry. He opened his mouth. He had a large amount of blood in his mouth. I thought I saw a chunk of flesh in his mouth, but I was mistaken. He hugged Keith and apologized. Keith was crying and told him it was okay.

Keith and the gay Indian both had bloody noses, scratches, bumps, bruises, and torn clothing. The apartment was a mess from the three of them fighting. As Keith was being loaded in the ambulance, he looked at me and said, "Hey, McMann, don't tell all your homo cop friends about this." I smiled.

When Trip was still in diapers but could speak clearly, I taught him his first cuss word when we were home alone. I was putting clothes away and noticed he was in the kitchen. I also noticed he appeared to be working a good poo. His face was red, and he had a serious look on his face. I walked by a few minutes later and noticed he was still squatting. I walked passed him a third time, and he had finished pooing. It was runny and had oozed out the back, front, and down his legs. There was some on the kitchen floor, which he was using to

Move Along; Nothing to See Here

finger paint. I looked at him and said, "Dammit." I didn't say it loudly. I thought I said it to myself like, "Wow, what a mess." He looked at me for about ten seconds and said, "Dammit." I said, "No, Daddy said darn it." He said, "Dammit dammit dammit."

I put him in the bathtub. He said, "Dammit, Daddy." I said, "No, Trip. Daddy said darn it. Dammit is a bad word." It took me about twenty minutes to convince him that I said darn it. I cleaned up the kitchen floor and listened the rest of the day to see if he would say it again. He didn't.

The next night we got home from church, and Trip was in the living room with me while I was watching Sunday Night Baseball on ESPN. He was standing next to me while I was sitting in my chair. When I looked at him, he said, "Dammit dammit dammit." I said, "No, Trip. Daddy said darn it. Dammit is a bad word." He said, "Daddy said dammit." It took me another thirty minutes to convince him I didn't say dammit. He finally said, "Daddy, dammit is a bad word." I said, "That's right, and we don't say that word." He eventually forgot how to say it. He would run around the house saying, "Jammit." I eventually convinced him not to say that either.

I responded to a disturbance at the residence of the grand poobah of the Sanders Beach Neighborhood Association. When I arrived I found a white male "unconscious" in the middle of Cypress Street. I called for EMS, and they transported him to the hospital. I contacted the grand poobah. He told me that he and the unconscious gentleman had a disagreement over how the neighborhood association was being operated. The conversation became heated, and he told the unconscious gentleman to leave. They shoved each other a couple of times. The unconscious gentleman walked out to the street, called the police, and passed out just before you arrived. I contacted the unconscious gentleman at the hospital who told me basically the same thing. He told me the grand poobah followed him out to the street and punched him in the back of his head, knocking him unconscious. I asked, "Are you sure that's what happened?" He nodded yes. I said, "I saw you from at least five blocks away. You were looking to

Darrell McMann

the west. You turned and noticed, I was coming. You looked around and then lay down in the street." He didn't say anything for a minute. He said, "He hit me while we were arguing on his front porch. I walked out to the street and collapsed." I said, "So when did you call 911?" He said, "I called 911 and then collapsed." I said, "How did your cell phone get in your pocket?" He said, "I must have put in my pocket as I was collapsing." I said, "I have seen many people pass out over the years. I have never seen anyone drop to their knees and then lower themselves to a prone position on the ground. I saw you from five blocks away. You turned, saw me, and decided you were going to pass out. Do you still want to stick with your story?" He said, "No, forget it."

The house across the street from us is a rental property. A family moved in about a year or so after our house was finished. They had a little girl Elizabeth's age that had a bad habit of walking into the house without knocking if the garage door was up. I was sitting in my chair one Saturday afternoon watching TV. She walked into the living room and stood in front of my chair. She said, "I want something to drink." She had a fruit drink in her hand. I said, "Don't you have something to drink at home?" She said, "Yeah." I said, "Then go home and ask your momma for something to drink and don't come in here again without knocking." She said, "Okay" and didn't do it again.

Her brother was trouble from the beginning. The family had an ATV in the garage. He would get on it when his parents were gone and drive around the house like he was racing. There were ruts in the yard all the way around the house. The neighbors were gone one day when he rode up their driveway and ran into their garage door. His parents paid for a replacement. He hung out sometimes with the boy that lived next to him. I guess he got bored one day and found a marker; while the neighbors were gone he wrote on all the windows telling the neighborhood how gay the boy was. The neighbors were fit to be tied; I talked to him, but it didn't do any good.

One Saturday night Cindy took our dogs out, and she saw him climb out of his window and meet up with a couple of other kids in

Move Along; Nothing to See Here

the street. Cindy called his mother. His dad drove down the street a few minutes later and brought him home.

A few weeks later I raised the garage door to take Elizabeth to the ER. She had a high temperature we couldn't break. When the door opened, I detected the unmistakable aroma of marijuana. Dummy was sitting in a vehicle at the end of our driveway, fifty feet from my cruiser, on the opposite side of the street with three other guys smoking pot. They fell over themselves trying to put it out and then get into the house. I said, "HEY, YOU MUST THINK I'M STUPID!" He ignored me and kept walking. I yelled, "STOP!" They stopped. I said, "You are very lucky that I have to go to the ER. Don't ever do that again. I will talk to your parents next time I see them." He nodded and walked inside.

I came home later that night and saw that they were just getting home. I walked over carrying Trip who was about one-year-old at the time. I asked, "Has your son talked to you?" His mom said, "No, what has he done this time?" I told them what happened. His dad said, "Why didn't you arrest him?" I told them I was headed to the ER when it happened. Then I said, "I shouldn't have to worry about arresting people when I am at home. I'm telling you about it so you can take care of the problem." He just looked at me like I was stupid, so I went home.

A couple of days later I walked out and smelled marijuana again. I looked down the street and noticed a truck parked in front of the house next door. Knucklehead was in the passenger seat smoking with a buddy; I started walking toward him. The closer I got the more concerned he looked. I opened his door and told him to get out. While I was searching him, his buddy said, "You can't do that." I said, "Shut your mouth, idiot. You're next." I walked over and opened the door and searched him too. Knucklehead said, "I thought it would be okay because I'm not in front of your house." I said, "Please tell me you aren't that stupid." Neither one of them said anything else. I didn't find any grass on them or in the truck. Christmas was approaching, and I was taking the week off between Christmas and New Year's. I was

Darrell McMann

going to leave my cruiser at the city garage to have some work done on it, so I said, "Just because my cruiser may not be in my driveway doesn't mean I am not home." Knucklehead said, "But it's parked there now, and you are home." I said, "That's pretty observant."

New Year's Eve I walked out the front door to take the trash out. I heard loud music coming from down the street. Before I could tell where it was coming from, my neighbor said, "Can you please have knucklehead turn that crap down!" I smiled and threw my trash away. I started walking toward him and the two vehicles that were playing the music; there were seven guys with him. I was wearing shorts and a T-shirt. I said, "Would ya'll mind turning that down?" They turned it down. I said, "I know ya'll aren't going to hang out right here all night." One of his buddies said, "What if we don't leave? What are you going to do about it?" Before I could answer, Knucklehead said, "He's a cop." His buddy said, "Where's your gun and badge?" I said, "They are in the house. Would it make you feel better if I went and got them? And to answer your previous question, if I can't get you to leave, I know I can have someone come help me." One of them said, "What's your name. I am going to make a complaint about you." I said, "Would you like my business card? That way you won't have to remember." He said, "Are you saying I'm stupid?" I said, "I'm just trying to be helpful." He said, "We will leave. We were about to go anyway." I said, "Ya'll be careful tonight." One of them said, "Yeah, you, too." I said, "If you are going to threaten me, just go ahead and do it." He said, "Oh, I'm not threatening you. I'm sorry if you took it that way." They left.

I was at work one afternoon around 5:00 P.M., when someone noticed a couple of teenagers smoking a joint as they were driving down Garden Street heading toward downtown; they gave a description of the vehicle, and I saw it a couple of minutes later. I noticed that the passenger looked back at me and then looked like he was trying to hide something. I stopped the car and found a dime bag on the driver. I thought I recognized the passenger. When I checked his ID, I saw that he lived near me. I remembered seeing him at Knucklehead's house. I asked him if he knew Knucklehead. He said he did. He said, "Don't you live across the street from him?" I said, "Yeah and I don't

Move Along; Nothing to See Here

want to see you over there." He said, "Don't worry. You got Knuckle-head scared to death."

I called the passenger's parents to come pick him up. When they showed up they were in shock that their baby boy could have possibly been involved in anything illegal. They almost made it sound like I was making it up. I showed them what I found and then asked if they had seen his wallet. His wallet had a marijuana leaf sewn on the outside. They were in shock and became extremely upset when I showed them the roach clip he carried.

A couple weeks later Cindy was outside the house when she heard a terrible racket coming from the street. She looked out to the street and noticed Knucklehead walking away from the storm drain. She looked in the storm drain and saw a case of beer bottles. She told me, and I walked over and knocked on Knucklehead's door. He was home alone and opened the door. I said, "Why did you dump your empty beer bottles in the drain?" He said, "I didn't" I interrupted him and said, "You were seen dumping them in there. Don't lie to me." He said, "Sorry," and closed the door. I felt somewhat satisfied and went home.

Knucklehead kept a low profile for the next seven or eight months. He was expelled from high school and wasn't spending too much time at home. I found out he was arrested by the sheriff's office with two of his buddies when they beat up some kid and took his jacket; one of them threatened the kid with a gun. That night I noticed he had several visitors. The next day I went to the state attorney's office to find out if there were provisions in place for him to be released. I found out he could only be outside if he was supervised by one of his parents. He couldn't have any friends over unless he was supervised by one of his parents, and there were several other stipulations. I typed a letter to his parents indicating everything I discovered at the state attorney's office. I intended to ensure that he was following all the rules; I put it in their mail box. That night I saw Knucklehead was in the front yard with his dad; they both glared at me. I guess they were mad because now they had to spend time together.

Darrell McMann

I usually string Christmas lights along the front of the house the week after Thanksgiving. I was on the ladder when I looked down the street and noticed a thug walking down the street. I stared at him, but he was doing all he could not to look at me. He stopped in front Knucklehead's house and stared at the front door; he answered his cell phone. I heard him say, "Hold on, I'll look." He turned and looked at me real quick. He said, "Yeah, he's looking at me." He said, "Okay" and walked back in the direction he came from.

A couple of weeks later I was standing in my garage when a couple of his thug-for-life buddies drove up in the driveway. I could see his dad sitting in the window while they hung out in the driveway playing rap music, with their saggy pants, sideways ball caps, and their hands down the front of their pants. I walked over and said, "I don't live in the hood. If you want to play the part of a hood rat, go to the hood. I don't want to see it." He got mad and walked in the house and they left.

A couple days later I was in the front yard with Trip and Elizabeth. Three cars heading north were stopped at the stop sign in front of our house. The first car was making a left turn to go west but had to wait for a car approaching from the east. A small red truck turned into the neighborhood off of Ten Mile Road. The truck went around all three cars stopped at the stop sign and forced the driver of the car to slam on his brakes as it made the turn. The truck barely came to a stop when Knucklehead jumped out in front of his house. His buddy squealed his tires when he drove away. I said, "Tell your buddy, I owe him a ticket." He said, "Tell him yourself." I said, "I'm not your dad, and you aren't going to disrespect me." He walked into the house. He came out a few minutes later. He was talking on the phone to someone about me. I said, "Tell whoever you are talking to I said hello." He slammed the door when he went inside.

Just after 5:00 P.M. I answered the front door when the doorbell rang; it was his parents. His mother said, "We are tired of you harassing Knucklehead." I said, "If ya'll would have taken care of him like you should have from the beginning, I wouldn't have to spend so much

Move Along; Nothing to See Here

time jumping down his throat." They started defending him. I said, "I just put some pork chops on the grill. I gotta go." His dad turned and started walking down the driveway. I heard him say something, but I wasn't sure what he said. I said, "What was that?" He kept walking. I said, "That's what I thought." They moved the following weekend.

A couple of weeks later we finishing dinner at Cracker Barrel when I noticed the hostess escorting Knucklehead and his mom to a table next to ours. We made eye contact. Knucklehead's mom asked the hostess if they could sit somewhere else. They moved to the other side of the restaurant. I thought it was funny.

We started getting several calls a night about someone shining a high-powered flashlight in the eyes of drivers as they were stopped at traffic lights. A few people attempted to chase the suspect's vehicle, but he managed to get away. The suspects changed tactics and began shining the flashlight at people who were walking in the East Hill neighborhood. One old man pulled a gun from his van, and the suspects took off at a high rate of speed. He laughed because it wasn't loaded. No one thought to get the tag number or try to get a good description of the suspects. We finally found three boys aged sixteen to eighteen driving through East Hill with the flashlight in the backseat; we called their parents. I took the boy who was driving the car aside, and he admitted he was alone for most of the incidents. I told him he was in serious trouble. The FBI was investigating because some of the people they targeted were black. He asked, "Why?" I said, "They are calling it a hate crime. You are trying to deny them their Civil Rights." He started crying. I said, "They could also categorize what you have done as terrorism. Haven't you heard of the Patriot Act?" He started crying harder. I said, "You need to think about the gravity of your actions. I'm going to contact all the people you terrorized to see if they want to press charges. I'll get back with you in about a week."

When his dad showed up I told him what his son had been up to for the last two weeks and what I told his son. I told him there hadn't actually been any written reports, but I wanted him to believe there

Darrell McMann

was until I got back to him the following week. His dad loved how I handled it and told me he would go along with my story.

I called him the following week and left a message for him to call me. His mother called me about fifteen minutes later. She wasn't clued in on the story and thought the situation was resolved. His parents were divorced, which explains the communication breakdown. She said, "I don't appreciate you harassing my son. You have no business calling him. I am a schoolteacher and I know." I interrupted her. I said, "First of all I am not harassing your son. I don't think you are aware of what he was doing. Secondly, I don't care what or who you know." She said, "Well are you coming soon?" I said, "Just as soon as I'm finished with the complaint I'm working." She said, "You better get here soon because we are leaving." I said, "I'll be there as soon as I can." She hung up.

I had a trainee and I said, "This should be interesting." I said, "Don't say anything. I'm going to turn my microphone on for the camera." She answered the door and by the look on her face, I knew she was going to be trouble. She said, "Please sit down." We sat. She sat down on the other side of the room next to her son. She said, "I feel you are harassing my son, I think you are making a bigger deal out of it than you should." I asked her if she knew what he had been up to the previous two weeks. She said, "He has been at home." I said, "Did you ask him?" She didn't answer. I said, "I spoke to his father the other night. He understood that I had planned to speak with your son this week." She said, "WE ARE DIVORCED! WE DON'T PASS MESSAGES!" I informed her of the conversation I had with her ex-husband.

She said, "You are making my son out to be the worst criminal in Pensacola." I said, "No, I'm trying to get him to think about what he was doing. He scared women as they were walking, he scared people he "shined," and a few of them chased him. One man got out his gun. What he was doing was incredibly stupid." She said, "So, you are saying my son is incredibly stupid?" I said, "No ma'am, your son was *acting* incredibly stupid."

Move Along; Nothing to See Here

She said, "I don't think it was him." I said, "I would like to agree with you, but the incidents stopped when we found your son, and he admitted he that was doing it. You aren't doing him any favors by trying to protect him when I already know that he was responsible." I said, "There are no reports. None of the people he harassed wanted it documented. They just wanted us to find out who was doing it and make the person stop. I wanted him to think about what he did for a few days." She said, "WHO DO YOU THINK YOU ARE? You must be the judge, jury, and executioner." I stood up and said, "Obviously you refuse to listen to anything I have to say." We walked out while she was yelling at us.

Ten minutes later Sergeant Wilson called me. He said, "The mother of the kid that "shined" all those people in East Hill called me. She said you were very rude and disrespectful." I said, "I taped the conversation, Sarge." He said, "I will call her back and let her know." Sarge called me a few minutes later. He said, "I called her back and told her I asked you about your visit to her house." She said, "I bet he lied." He said, "No ma'am, he recorded the entire conversation. Would you still like to make a complaint?" She said, "JUST FORGET IT!" and hung up.

I entered a Vacation Getaway for two to the Bahamas at a car wash. I was notified a couple of months later that I had won. The room and the trip from Fort Lauderdale on the cruise ship to Freeport were paid for. I found the hotel's Web site online. It looked okay, but I noticed that all the pictures of the rooms were taken from a distance. We discovered why when we arrived. The hotel was pink, which we could tell by the pictures on the Web site. Also according to the Web site, all the rooms had a balcony that looked out over a picturesque bay.

We checked in and were given a room key. We were told to come back in an hour for an orientation meeting. We walked to the room and found the door and sliding glass doors were completely open. The door had a deadbolt but no knob. The bathroom needed a lot of TLC, but it wasn't nasty. The carpeting was fraying, and there were a couple places where you could see three or four inches of the floor. Bare wires ran down the walls from the ceiling. We were relieved that

Darrell McMann

the bed was clean. I stood on the balcony and tried to find the picturesque view of the bay, but I could only see brown, brackish water. We went to our meeting and had dinner. We were asked if we would go to a resort for a tour, free lunch, and then the sales pitch. We decided to go.

We had our own tour guide who was very nice. We had our free lunch, which was very good, and then the guide started her sales pitch. I told her it was a very nice place; it was a lot nicer than where we were staying, which is more than likely planned that way.

I asked her how much, and she came up with an amount. I told her it was too much. She came up with a lower number. That was still too much. She talked for a little longer and threw out another number. I didn't like that number either. She said, "I thought you said you liked it here. Were you lying?" I said, "If you come up with a price I like, we will think about it. And you don't know me well enough to question me." She apologized. She said, "I need to speak to my boss. I'll be right back." She came back with another price. I told her I could work with that, and we bought a time share. The resort paid for a taxi to take us back to our hotel to get our stuff. We moved into a room on the beach. We had a good time and watched some interesting people.

Chapter 17

Just before 5:00 P.M. one weekday night, the Santa Rosa County Sheriff's Office bolo'd (be on the lookout for) a vehicle. Several drivers called 911 about a driver who was speeding and driving erratically. A deputy briefly chased the car down highway 98 but called off the pursuit when the vehicle reached 100 miles per hour. The car was last seen heading west toward Pensacola. A few minutes later several people called 911 about the same vehicle speeding and driving erratically across the Three Mile Bridge. Once off the bridge the vehicle could go in one of three directions. North on Seventeenth Avenue, continue west on Gregory Street, or bear left and head west on Bayfront Parkway. I decided to go to Fourteenth and Gregory. If he went in one of the other two directions, I could get him quickly. Our lieutenant, Randy Easton, suggested we try to box him in. He also didn't want us chasing him during rush hour, and I wasn't excited about that either. Jerry Jones was waiting at Ninth and Gregory. We didn't have to wait very long.

The vehicle sped by me before I knew he was there. I got on the radio and advised Jerry he was going too fast for us to box him in. He was on top of Jerry as I was talking on the radio. The vehicle had to slow down for traffic stopped for the red light and that helped me catch up to him. He weaved his way through traffic and then turned north on Ninth Avenue, accelerating rapidly. Jerry and I both turned our emergency lights on. We wanted to follow him from a distance because it was too dangerous to chase him.

A car heading south on Ninth Avenue was making a left turn onto Gadsden Street, and the driver, not realizing how fast the maniac was going, turned into his path. Both vehicles spun in midair and were just coming to rest when we pulled up. Needless to say I was a tiny bit pissed. Jerry went to help the other vehicle. I jumped out of my cruiser and tried to open the suspect's driver side door, but it was damaged too badly for me to open. The suspect told me he was trapped. The

Move Along; Nothing to See Here

car started smoking as I ran around to the passenger side. I checked quickly and realized the car was overheated and wasn't on fire. Several people in the McDonalds parking lot were screaming at me to get away from the car, but they couldn't see what I was looking at. I opened the passenger door and several beer cans fell out into the gutter, which got me even angrier. I grabbed the suspect's right arm and tried to pull him out, but he was pinned in the vehicle. I found out later his right arm and left leg were broken. OOOPS! The two ladies who pulled into the suspect's path were going to the church at the corner of Ninth and Gadsden. The driver lost one of her legs below her knee.

An individual had tried for several days to contact a friend who was going through some tough times. He finally spoke to him on the phone, and his friend told him he couldn't take it anymore and wanted to end it all. The friend told dispatch his friend sounded very drunk. An officer was dispatched to the house. Ski responded also to assess the situation. Ski got the guy on the phone briefly, but he just cursed and hung up. Ski called me to see if I could speak with him.

When I arrived I couldn't find Ski right away, when I spotted him at the corner of the other end of the house, I decided to run in a crouch across the front of the house. I got about halfway when the front door burst open and a man stepped out on the porch. I stopped and drew my gun. He yelled, "WHO THE HELL KEEPS CALLING MY PHONE?" He looked at me and yelled, "WAS IT YOU?" He was very animated and was only wearing a pair of shorts, so I was fairly certain he wasn't armed. I said, "Your friend called us because he is worried about you. The sergeant called you to see if you are okay." He yelled, "YEAH, I'M WONDERFUL. HOW ABOUT YOU?" I said, "I guess I'm okay, but I would like to talk to you." He heard Ski's phone ringing and yelled, "WHERE IS THE SOB WITH THE PHONE? IS HE HIDING AROUND THE CORNER?" He saw Ski's foot and started screaming at Ski. I realized I was only ten feet away, which was more than close enough for my Taser. I decided I would try and end this quickly while he was busy screaming at Ski. I deployed my Taser, and the darts struck him in the chest. As the Taser was going through its five-second cycle we stood there and stared

Darrell McMann

at each other. I noticed he was tensing (5,000 volts will do that), but he didn't fall. When the five-second cycle ended, he screamed, "WHY IN THE HELL DID YOU DO THAT? THAT HURT!" Realizing I had made a mistake, I said, "I know, and I'm sorry. I tried to get this over quickly, but I was wrong." He yelled, "THAT FREAKING HURT!" As he was yelling at me, Sergeant Sonya Hunt had walked up and was standing behind a tree about ten feet from me. She was trying to get me to come behind the tree.

He noticed she was there and screamed, "WHAT IN THE HELL DOES SHE WANT? I said, "She's just looking out for me." Sonya said, "We just want to make sure you are okay and that no one gets hurt." He screamed, "IM NOT TALKING TO YOU. YOU NEED TO LEAVE GET THE HELL OUT OF HERE!" As Sonya walked back to her cruiser, he yelled, "I DON'T LIKE HER. SHE PISSED ME OFF!" I said, "I know how you feel. She pisses us off all the time. Just talk to me." He said, "Don't Tase me again. It hurt." I said, "I won't. I promise, and I'm sorry."

He started talking to me about how he was tired of living. He said, "I thought about shooting myself, but I couldn't do it." I knew I couldn't allow him to go back in the house, so we started talking about what was bothering him. By now I was standing about a foot from the porch and could see Henry Dent out of the corner of my eye crawling over the railing on the side of the porch. The guy put both hands on top of the railing looking over me and bent down to me. He said, "I'm tired, and I'm ready to end this." I thought about grabbing his wrists and pulling him over the railing, but I knew Henry was about to tackle him. I said, "Take it easy, and everything will be fine." Henry tackled him a few seconds later. We cuffed him real quick and checked the house. There were beer bottles laying everywhere. He didn't have a gun in the house, but I suspect he was going to try to make one of us shoot him. We took him to the hospital to be evaluated. I never heard anything more from him.

I responded to one of the downtown hotels one evening. The staff overheard two of the guests talking about finding some cocaine and prostitutes. The manager wanted me to ask them to leave. I told him

Move Along; Nothing to See Here

I might need him to come to the room. He agreed and I went to the room. I knocked on the door and heard movement in the room. The guy who opened the door obviously wasn't expecting a police officer. Sgt Wilson joined me as I started talking to him.

I said, "The manager of the hotel has some concerns about you and your friend. Where is your friend?" He said, "He left." I saw two freshly opened beer bottles sitting on the night stand. I said, "Who is in here with you?" He said, "I'm alone. My buddy left." I asked him for his ID. He reached for his back pocket and then suddenly bolted toward one of the beds. I got to him just as he was reaching for something and grabbed him by the back of his shirt. I pulled him back into a chair. I said, "What are you doing?" He said, "Getting my wallet." I said, "Where is your friend?" He said, "He went home."

I looked on the floor and noticed a pair of jeans that seemed to be several sizes to large for him. I said, "Did ya'll have fight? He left his pants." I was halfway into the room when I saw movement out of the corner of my eye from the bathroom. I turned and saw a man in his underwear raising his right arm—there was a gun in his hand. I pulled my gun and yelled, "DROP IT!" He tossed it on the bed. I ordered him to the floor. He began to argue with me, but I convinced him to do what I asked. As I cuffed him, he said, "I am a retired Montgomery, Alabama, police captain." I cuffed him and asked him if he knew how close he had been to dying. He ignored that and said, "Look in my wallet. My ID and my credentials are in there." I looked, and he was a retired Montgomery PD captain, and he had a pistol permit. He said, "You take these off." I ignored him. I said, "Why did you come out of the bathroom with a gun in your hand?" He said, "I didn't know you were the police." I said, "You must not have been much of a cop. You heard the whole conversation and didn't know we were the police? I don't believe it. I think you were expecting a coke dealer. You were going to rob him or make sure you didn't get robbed." He didn't say anything.

The sarge told them the hotel wanted them to leave. The retired captain said, "Do I get my gun back?" I said, "Gather your junk and

Darrell McMann

meet me in the parking lot." They described their truck. They came out to the parking lot, and he said, "Give me my gun back." I told him to open the truck. When he did I tossed the bullets under the back seat and set the gun on top of the backseat. I said, "I suggest you wait until you leave before you reload your gun." I walked away, and they left.

In September of 2008 one of Elizabeth's friends at school told her she was getting messages on MySpace from a girl in Alabama. She was asking questions about Elizabeth. She didn't tell her anything. Elizabeth had a MySpace account that we monitored. Cindy found my niece's page and sent her a message. They exchanged messages for a couple days, and the cousin wrote that her grandparents were in poor health. Cindy said, "We should go see them." I thought about it for minute and decided to give them another chance. Maybe time had changed them.

We arranged to meet them at Kim's sister's house on a weekend in November. We met them and everything went very well. Elizabeth was extremely nervous, and who could blame her? Surprisingly, I felt pretty good about it. We spent the day together, and that night Elizabeth went to the skating rink with her cousin.

Kim's sister and her daughter came to Pensacola a couple of times and visited with us. Everything seemed to be fine. We went to Kim's sister's house the first Saturday after Christmas; they had purchased gifts for Trip and Elizabeth. Elizabeth was going to spend the night in with Kim's parents. Cindy and I were nervous about it, but we agreed to do it anyway. Elizabeth came home and told us her grandparents were kind of quiet and went to bed early. She wasn't totally comfortable around them.

Kim's sister called and wanted to get Elizabeth every other weekend. I said, "I know you want to make up for lost time, but you have to remember that we have a life. We are busy with school, church, family, and friends. I want ya'll to be a part of her life, but you need to be patient and understand that." She seemed to accept that. Kim's sister sent Cindy an e-mail about Elizabeth spending the weekend

Move Along; Nothing to See Here

with them and gave her a date. Cindy replied that for right now, Elizabeth wasn't going anywhere because she was being hard headed and disrespectful. Cindy suggested that we would see how she was in a couple of weeks; she mentioned a weekend three weeks away if Elizabeth's behavior improved. Cindy mentioned she had been nervous about Elizabeth spending the night with her parents before she went but felt better about it now.

That Saturday night at 10:30 P.M. Kim's mother called and asked for me. She was upset about the e-mail. She said, "Why isn't Elizabeth allowed to come see us?" I had no idea what she is talking about. Cindy showed the e-mail to me, and I read it to Kim's mother. I said, "You are focusing on the part about her not going anywhere. It doesn't specify a place. She got in trouble, so we are not allowing her to go anywhere for a couple of weeks. I don't know how you came up with the idea it was focusing on any of you. You completely missed the sentence stating what weekend we would shoot for." Instead of apologizing she said, "The e-mail upset me." I said, "You should have read the whole thing." She asked to speak to Cindy.

When she got Cindy on the phone she asked, "Did you adopt Elizabeth?" Cindy told her it was none of her business. Then she said, "When I see Elizabeth, I don't need to see you. What kind of Christian women are you? You are not her mother, and you aren't blood related." Cindy handed me the phone. I got back on the phone, but she had decided she didn't want to speak anymore and hung up.

I called her Monday night. In a low, monotone voice I said, "It was Cindy's idea to get in touch with ya'll. You should thank her. I will not tolerate her being spoken to like that. I realize you were upset by the e-mail, but you didn't read the whole message. Don't ever question her Christianity. She got me back in church, and Elizabeth is saved. You owe Cindy an apology." She hung up. I stared at the phone for a few seconds and laughed.

Kim's sister called me the next morning on my cell phone. She asked, "Are you trying to kill my mother?" I said, "WHAT?" She told me

Darrell McMann

her mother had a spell; they almost had to take her to the hospital because I was yelling and cussing at her on the phone, and she said that they had recorded it.

I said, "You mean to tell me she can call us late at night and bitch at us over her stupidity, and she doesn't have a spell, but I calmly tell her she owes Cindy an apology, and she has a fit? That's crazy stupid." She said, "One day I will tell Elizabeth all about you." I said, "Elizabeth was in the kitchen Saturday night while we were talking to your mom. She knows exactly what was said. She was twenty feet from me when I talked to your mom about apologizing to Cindy. She already knows the truth. I know you think I have done nothing but talk about ya'll for the past nine years. I haven't—I have better things to do than dwell on your trash." I then went on a five-minute profanity -laced rant that made me feel better but also made feel convicted. I didn't regret jumping down her throat but I didn't like the fact that I went on an "F" bomb dropping rampage. I don't like that word. When intelligent people use it they sound ignorant and ignorant people sound stupid.

Other than that life is good.

Made in the USA
Lexington, KY
13 September 2010